# Replicating Dreams

A Comparative Study of
Grameen Bank and its replication,
Kashf Foundation, Pakistan

# Replicating Dreams

## A Comparative Study of Grameen Bank and its replication, Kashf Foundation, Pakistan

### NABIHA SYED

**OXFORD**
UNIVERSITY PRESS

# OXFORD
UNIVERSITY PRESS

Great Clarendon Street, Oxford OX2 6DP

Oxford University Press is a department of the University of Oxford.
It furthers the University's objective of excellence in research, scholarship,
and education by publishing worldwide in

Oxford   New York

Auckland  Cape Town  Dar es Salaam  Hong Kong  Karachi
Kuala Lumpur  Madrid  Melbourne  Mexico City  Nairobi
New Delhi  Shanghai  Taipei  Toronto

with offices in

Argentina  Austria  Brazil  Chile  Czech Republic  France  Greece
Guatemala  Hungary  Italy  Japan  Poland  Portugal  Singapore
South Korea  Switzerland  Turkey  Ukraine  Vietnam

Oxford is a registered trade mark of Oxford University Press
in the UK and in certain other countries

ISBN  978-0-19-547652-1

Typeset in Adobe Garamond Pro
Printed in Pakistan by
Mehran Printers, Karachi.
Published by
Ameena Saiyid, Oxford University Press
No. 38, Sector 15, Korangi Industrial Area, PO Box 8214
Karachi-74900, Pakistan.

# Contents

# Acknowledgements

I would like to extend special thanks to Johns Hopkins University for the grant of the Robins Fellowship because of which I was able to obtain the academic basis and the financial support required to undertake this project. I would also like to thank Amnesty International for the Patrick Stewart Scholarship which allowed for travel, research and resources in Pakistan.

I am also deeply grateful for the help, guidance and hospitality I received from: Mr Fazli Rabbi, Mrs Jannat-e-Quanine, Farzana Kashfi, Noorjehan Begum, Feroze Fakhri, Nourredine Khallouki, Faisal Malik, Sameen Shahid, Justice Majida Rizvi, Mr Alamgir, Farida Shaheed and the Malik family; and finally, my deep gratitude to my own family for their support and encouragement. Thank you so much for an extraordinary experience. This report would not have been possible without your help.

# INTRODUCTION

**M**icrocredit has been widely lauded as a viable, practical solution for alleviating poverty throughout the world: following the UN's recognition of the International Year of Microcredit 2005 and the award of the Nobel Peace Prize to Professor Muhammad Yunus in 2006, microcredit has emerged as a prominent and key component of development strategy. Replications of the award-winning Grameen Bank Solidarity Group Lending Model have proliferated throughout the world, with over 200 replications to date. But how do these replications translate in different contexts? How do they negotiate the demands of different environments? And are these replications experiencing the same sort of widespread success for which Grameen has become famous?

I focus on one Grameen replication in particular: the Kashf Foundation in Pakistan. With 10 million adults, considered financially eligible for microcredit assistance, Pakistan is one of the world's largest potential microcredit markets. Kashf is the most successful Grameen replication in the country, and is also widely recognized as one of the leaders of microfinance in Pakistan. General similarities in culture, religion and shared history imply that environmental differences between Bangladesh and Pakistan would not be hugely excessive, or worthy of major alteration. I researched with Grameen Bank and the Kashf Foundation in 2005 to understand environmental differences and the consequent institutional changes between the original and the replication. This study is by no means an exhaustive examination of microfinance in Pakistan as a whole, as that would require an analysis of individual lending programmes, rural support lending programmes, microleasing institutions, and the like. Instead, this introduces the basic structure of both Grameen and

Kashf, analyses their institutional differences, and then conceptualizes outreach in a shifting microcredit market as a means of achieving empowerment.

The success of microcredit is attributed to its ability to reach the 'double bottom line'; that is, its ability to actualize both financial and social empowerment. Empowerment, though ambiguous in its definition, can be evaluated by the ability to grant women a sense of agency in their daily lives. The idea of 'successful' microcredit, then, is one which combines effective outreach with empowerment of those agents who have taken part in the programme. I define success as the achievement of the double bottom line, and then look at factors which might adversely affect this goal in these approaches to the Solidarity Group Lending Model

This study is divided into two major sections. The first section is a depiction of both institutions, with detailed descriptions of their operating style. To elucidate the particularities of each model, I will look at their general tenets, eligibility requirements, services offered, and general organizational model. After establishing these characteristics, I will then compare their general success in outreach. This will be followed by an elaboration on Kashf and Grameen's distinctive institutional, environmental and socio-political settings, and how these may translate into barriers to increased outreach. Importantly, these factors are merely an overview of potential issues to consider. I hope that the introduction of some of these factors may prompt and inspire others to engage in more extensive research on the individual issues introduced here.

In the second section, I argue that tailored outreach models engaging in a depth-oriented rather than breadth-oriented microcredit market can ultimately result in the flourishing of individual and aggregate social empowerment. I look at marketing as a means of establishing a market-responsive outreach method, enhancing both institutional efficiency and trust. Furthermore, I examine the instrumental role of branding in facilitating these key values. Ultimately, I conclude that institutions engaging in depth-oriented, market-responsive models can profitably build on new forms of social capital into whole-scale social activism. A conceptualization of empowerment as choice-freedom is instrumental to this end.

CHAPTER ONE
# Grameen Group Lending Model Overview

Microcredit outreach in Bangladesh is wildly successful: the market penetration is estimated to be over 75 per cent of poor, eligible and willing families. Bangladeshi microcredit programmes are lauded for enhancing the welfare of both participants and non-participants alike by increasing aggregate welfare at the village level. In this way, microcredit programmes have a greater impact on extreme poverty than on moderate poverty.[1] Internal studies conducted by Grameen Bank show that 42 per cent of borrowing families eventually cross the poverty line, demonstrating a dramatic improvement in ten indicator areas including size, savings amount, housing condition and availability of necessities such as warm clothing.[2] Through the Grameen Bank Replication Programme, Grameen group-lending style programmes have been replicated across the world. Of over 200 replications, however, none has achieved the market penetration success achieved by its predecessor; Muhammad Yunus, founder of Grameen Bank, attributes this to a lack of capacity to extend outreach.

Surely the Grameen model cannot be blamed for its complexity: its appeal lies in the simple yet effective method of disbursing loans to those who demonstrate a need and desire for self-motivated entrepreneurship. Understanding that the poorest of the poor have been excluded from access to financial services, Grameen's Solidarity Group Lending Model uses social collateral to ensure weekly repayment of small loans usually less than $100 in size. Small loans are distributed individually to women organized into groups of five; each woman is responsible for not only her own repayment but also the repayment of others in her group, as any outstanding debt precludes grant of future loans to other members of the group. The Solidarity Group Lending Model thus utilizes collective responsibility to ensure repayment.

'Grameen credit', as Muhammad Yunus terms the model, has specific targets which distinguish it from other financial programmes. The primary mission of Grameen credit is to help families help themselves to overcome poverty: its intention is to create 'self-employment for income-generating activities and housing, as opposed to consumption.' Grameen credit aims to promote the skills of the poor which remain 'unutilized or under-utilized', in order to bring them out of poverty by 'unleashing [their] energy and creativity to answer poverty.'[3] Emphasizing that individuals must follow their own entrepreneurial spirit, Grameen does not offer job training or career building services. Instead, the emphasis is on building social capital by incorporating women into a system which stresses leadership and self-initiative. Grameen conceptualizes credit as an essential human right, and is driven by the passionate conviction that poverty is not created by the poor but rather by institutions and policies which surround them. Pitt and Khandker underscore this notion in their examination of individual and household outcomes in Bangladesh, concluding that access to credit is a significant determinant of many household outcomes.[4]

## WHO IS ELIGIBLE?

Grameen caters to the rural landless who qualify as the poorest of the poor. This means that their lack of collateral has disqualified them from traditional financial services. Qualifying as landless means that one possesses less than half an acre of land or assets that amount to less than the value of an acre of medium quality land; this definition encompasses approximately half the rural population of Bangladesh.[5] To possess less than a half-acre indicates that the potential client has few resources or outlets for income generation. As such, financial assistance in the form of credit access can provide acutely needed help, more so because other credit options are either extortionate or simply unavailable.

Grameen's unique model addresses the issue of collateral when dealing with the destitute. This demographic has been denied access to financial institutions because they have no collateral to ensure repayment of a traditional loan. The high opportunity cost of fortnightly meetings and the small amount of loan makes the Grameen system unappealing to large farmers and the rural rich, effectively excluding them from the programme. The demographic targeted then is systematically narrowed to the landless and the destitute.

To guarantee payment, Grameen developed a Solidarity Group Lending Model in which groups of five are assembled to use peer monitoring and social collateral to enforce repayment and efficient monitoring of the business. High-risk borrowers are screened out of the process, as in a village environment a reputation for unreliability would preclude a person's inclusion in a lending group that is jointly liable for all members. If one member of the group defaults on a loan, all are penalized for the lapse. Either all other group members will have to cover the cost of the defaulted loan or face the prospect of being excluded from future borrowing. Group members are thus given a strong motivation to not only help one another, but also ensure repayment and proper conduct as per the rules of Grameen Bank. Peer monitoring reduces transaction costs of the primary institution by placing it in the hands of the social pressure mechanism.

The groups are self-selected and must be homogenous in their gender composition. Although men and women both have opportunities to join, women have dominated the process and now take 97 per cent of all loans. Group members cannot be related in any manner, must be from the same village and must have similar social and economic backgrounds to prevent unequal bargaining strength within the group. Upon selecting a suitable group, the members are sorted into centres consisting of five groups each. The process of screening now begins: members are required to attend meetings for fourteen days during which they must learn to sign their name, learn about Grameen's objectives and memorize Grameen's Sixteen Decisions for 'healthy' social behaviour. Discipline is greatly emphasized during this training, with the assigned loan officer testing and quizzing members to ensure their suitability for the programme. Loans are disbursed only when the loan officer is satisfied with the knowledge of all members of each group; as a result, the group model creates incentive for cooperative learning. Moreover, the training fosters close relationships amongst group members as well as centre members. In creating a strong social network, women involved in the centre can support one another in what will be, for many, their first entrepreneurial venture.

Self-selection and peer monitoring are the two salient features which allow the Solidarity Group Lending Model to work. The former, however, may interestingly work to the detriment of what Syed Hashemi terms the 'hard core poor'. There are differences in the magnitude of poverty, a phenomenon complicating effective targeting of the most impoverished. The 'hard core poor' are those who are 'forced to subsist on a per capita income that is less than half that of the poverty line;'[6] this group often self-selects itself out of Grameen participation only because they do not consider themselves creditworthy. The hard-core poor shy away from accumulating debt as they believe they do not have enough resources to generate repayment. This risk-aversion prevents their participation with Grameen. Out of 313 target-group households interviewed in Rangpur and Faridpur, 120 women had chosen not to participate: fifty-five thought they would not be able to manage the money and thus would incur more debt; thirty-five felt that leaving home to attend Grameen meetings in which males would be present violate social norms; eleven were rejected for being high-risk or having high-risk husbands; and nineteen said the rules were too complicated to understand and they were unable to memorize the Sixteen Decisions.[7] This observation of the self-selection bias is important in that it indicates that microfinance must be tailored to suit perceptions of individuals within a target group. Encouraging confidence and optimism regarding one's self-sufficiency is a prerequisite for the success of a microfinance programme hinged upon self-initiative.

For those who do choose to participate in a Grameen programme and are able to find four other co-borrowers to testify to their creditworthiness and reliability, the following services are offered:

**General Loan:** The General Loan of Bangladeshi Taka (Tk) 1000 is disbursed to women for entrepreneurial activities with a 20 per cent declining interest rate. The loans are entirely financed from the Bank's own deposits with over 64 per cent deposits coming from the Bank's own borrowers.

**Housing Loan:** Introduced in 1984, housing loans are provided to encourage the construction of strengthened houses with good sanitation. Many villagers live in makeshift shanties prone to toppling in severe weather; the Housing Loan promotes building safe, permanent habitation. The maximum amount disbursed is Tk 15,000 with the amount to be repaid in weekly instalments over a period of five years at 8 per cent interest; the average housing loan is approximately Tk 13,000. To date, 647,130 houses have been built using this loan with Tk 8.53 billion disbursed for this purpose. In the period from June 2006 to May 2007, 12,545 houses were built with loans amounting to Tk 133.47 million.

**Emergency Loan:** The Emergency Loan can be granted in times of distress or other demonstrable emergency. Qualifying situations include payment for household necessities and medical fees. Loan officers use their discretion to determine whether a given situation is an emergency and merits incurring additional debt.

**Struggling Members Programme:** Specifically targeting the hard-core poor, Grameen has expanded its services to include the Struggling Members Programme. The Programme disperses small loans to beggars with a completely flexible and optional repayment term. No interest is charged and members are covered under life and loan insurance programmes. The Programme specifically targets those who self-select out of participation in Grameen's more mainstream programmes because they lack entrepreneurial resources or confidence in their entrepreneurial abilities. Each Struggling Member is given an identity badge inscribed with the Grameen Bank logo in order to bolster confidence through identification with a national institution. Enabling beggars to sell small goods is thought to motivate an entrepreneurial spirit and stimulate self-esteem. Approximately 94,000 beggars have already joined the programme with disbursed amount standing at Tk 92.62 million. Of that amount, Tk 60.21 million has already been repaid.

**Microenterprise Loan:** These larger loans are granted to borrowers with significant business know-how, with no maximum amount specified. Borrowers of the microenterprise loan must have demonstrable credit reliability, often through the prior use of a General Loan. The funds are used to purchase merchandise such as irrigation pumps, transport and other equipment not accessible due to restricted amounts offered in the smaller loan. Thus far 1,085,959 members have taken these larger loans with Tk 23.42 billion disbursed. The average loan size is Tk 21,566 with the largest loan being Tk 1.2 million.

**Education Loans:** Children of parents who are involved with Grameen are given education loans which cover tuition, maintenance and other school expenses provided that they have reached the tertiary level of education. The Higher Education Loan has served 16,608 children as of May 2007.

## ORGANIZATIONAL MODEL

Grameen's efficiency lies in its decentralization. The transparent, simple system of loan disbursement delegates decision-making powers to the lowest relevant level, whether that is the branch, centre or group. The group-lending process nullifies the often high transaction costs associated with targeting a lower socioeconomic demographic, such as constant monitoring in case of impending default. Grameen is able to maintain a large target size because the group-lending process not only encourages peer monitoring as a means of repayment enforcement but also because the screening process is no longer entirely concentrated in the hands of the bank. Shifting the time-intensive burden of the screening process to the client substantially reduces transaction cost and labour.

Weekly meetings enhance the transparency of loan disbursement, emphasizing their regular and public nature. The centre meeting allows for group problem-solving regarding repayment issues or business difficulties. Open discussion strengthens the social collateral of the group as well as the centre. Furthermore, the regularity of the weekly meeting creates an organizational structure in which loans are paid regularly, received continuously and simultaneously, and monitored consistently and transparently. This cuts down on messy, time-consuming efforts for repayment enforcement as the group and centre inherit this responsibility rather than Grameen as an institution. Corruption is also kept to a minimum by the weekly meeting: financial transactions take place in the presence of all borrowers and the rationale for granting or rejecting loan applications are openly discussed so the potential for bribery and preferential treatment is limited. Suspicion that such corrupt practices may occur is eliminated and encourages those relationships of mutual trust which are so vital to the function of the Group Lending Model.[8] This cultivates increased confidence in Grameen itself and allows Grameen's reputation to effectively attract more borrowers.

The weekly visits of the loan officer to the centre foster a close, personal rapport between lender and borrower, facilitating problem-solving and enhancing consistent transparency. Constant contact with the clients in their own communities also ensures a high level of familiarity with socio-cultural demands on, and the economic needs of, particular borrowers. This makes it possible to provide a tailor-made response to any difficulty that a borrower may confront. The design of the system permits a certain amount of flexibility in implementation, and as such the procedures of the programme are 'fine-tuned' by the staff to best suit their clients. Because of this decentralized system, minor problems such as issues of interference by husbands and family members can be addressed by the field staff effectively and quickly besides which other group members can participate in this problem-solving process. Furthermore, the transparency of the operating procedures instils a trust in the system that could not be earned were there not a decentralized, personalized method of monitoring.

Grameen's emphasis on self-sufficiency and initiative is visible even on the organizational level: branches are encouraged to become self-sufficient as soon as possible. Branches monitor the centre's behaviour and offer day-to-day contact with members. Area offices manage the branches and function under the auspices of zonal managers. Almost all major policy decisions are taken at zonal manager conferences in which extensive, critical assessments of performance and intensive deliberations occur. Each zone policy is thus geared towards managing the problems that occur in its own jurisdiction according to norms and cultural nuances in each. The ability of the staff to familiarize themselves and target the issues in their jurisdiction is reinforced by an intensive introductory training programme as well as in-service staff training intended to support 'a problem-solving culture [which] puts total trust in the creative potential of its staff and clientele in crisis management.'⁹

## APPROACH TO SOCIAL REFORM

Grameen's approach to social reform is embodied in the Sixteen Decisions: these are an example of a social development programme intertwined with microcredit delivery. Developed in 1984, the Sixteen Decisions are an integral part of Grameen Bank's mission: all potential and current borrowers are expected to memorize them, and adherence to the Decisions is monitored by the loan officer. Additionally, the loan officer is to explore in-depth one decision per week, reinforce its applicability in the borrowers' lives and answer their questions to that end. The decisions are:

1. We shall follow and advance the four principles of the Grameen Bank (discipline, unity, courage and hard work) in all walks of our lives.
2. We shall bring prosperity to our families.
3. We shall not live in dilapidated houses. We shall repair our houses and work towards constructing new houses at the earliest possible.
4. We shall grow vegetables all the year round. We shall eat plenty of them and sell the surplus.
5. During the planting seasons, we shall plant as many seedlings as possible.
6. We shall plan to keep our families small. We shall minimize our expenditures. We shall look after our health.
7. We shall educate our children and ensure that they can earn to pay for their education.
8. We shall always keep our children and the environment clean.
9. We shall build and use pit-latrines.

10. We shall drink tube-well water. If it is not available, we shall boil water or use alum.
11. We shall not take any dowry in our sons' weddings, neither shall we give any dowry in our daughters' weddings. We shall keep the centre free from the curse of dowry. We shall not practice child marriage.
12. We shall not inflict any injustice on anyone, neither shall we allow anyone to do so.
13. For higher income, we shall collectively undertake bigger investments.
14. We shall always be ready to help each other. If anyone is in difficulty, we shall all help them.
15. If we come to know of any breach of discipline in any centre, we shall all go there and help restore discipline.
16. We shall introduce physical exercise in all our centres. We shall take part in all social activities collectively.

The Sixteen Decisions are a social development agenda that places primary responsibility for implementation on members rather than on Grameen Bank; as such, the expenditure incurred by Grameen for this social development programme is minimal. The simple approach is easily understood by the participants and reinforced through regular recitation and discussion. Furthermore, they are closely tailored to the setting of rural Bangladesh by having tangible and specific demands rather than nebulous, ambiguous statements of principle.

# NOTES

1. Syed M. Hashemi and Sidney Ruth Schuler, *Sustainable Banking With the Poor: A Case Study of Grameen Bank* (Grameen Trust: Dhaka, 2002):55.
2. *Grameen Performance Summary*, 2003. Provided by Grameen Trust on 18 June 2005.
3. H.I. Latifee, 'Microfinance and Poverty Reduction: Experiences of Grameen Operation in Asia'. Presented at Asian Regional Conference, 27–30 November 2000.
4. Mark Pitt and S.R. Khandker, 'Household and Intrahousehold Impact of the Grameen Bank and Similar Targeted Credit Programs in Bangladesh'. World Bank Working Paper Series (Washington, DC: World Bank, 1996).
5. Ahmed Rahman, 'Micro-credit Initiatives for Equitable and Sustainable Development: Who Pays?', *World Development Journal* (Vol. 27, 1999).
6. Syed M. Hashemi, 'Rural Credit Programs and Women's Empowerment in Bangladesh', *World Development Journal* (Vol. 24, No. 4, 1996).
7. Pitt and Khandker, op. cit., 14.
8. Latifee, op. cit., 44.
9. M.A. Chen, *Beyond Credit: A Subsector Approach to Promoting Women's Enterprises* (Canada: Aga Khan Foundation, 1996).

# Chapter Two
# Kashf Lending Model Overview

Established by a grant from the Grameen Trust in 1996, the Kashf Foundation is the most successful replication of the Solidarity Group Lending approach in Pakistan: its outreach as of June 2006 is estimated to be 136,015 active clients and 250 staff members in thirty centres in the Punjab region. At the time of this research in 2005, there were 75,520 active borrowers with an average loan balance of $187 per borrower. Of the thirty branches, I concentrated my efforts in the Lahore district: specifically, my research included field time in Bedian, Ravi Rayon, Yakki Gate and Chongi.

Though a multitude of other microfinance services exist in Pakistan (notably the First Woman's Bank, the Microfinance Bank, Khushali Bank, the National Rural Support Programme), Kashf is particularly unique in that it exists outside of state or quasi-state infrastructure. Importantly, Kashf is one of two NGOs in Pakistan seen as self-sustaining in their microcredit services. Kashf's methodology hinges on the utility of social capital as collateral, loaning exclusively to women in an initiative to empower women. Kashf's mission statement, as printed in a Department for International Development, UK (DFID) evaluation in 2003, is 'to provide quality and cost effective microfinance services to the poor rural, urban, and peri-urban women, focusing on adding value to their existing economic activities in order to enhance their economic roles both as autonomous decision-makers and as direct contributors to family income; and through a sustained increase in client incomes, it attempts to enable them to move out of the poverty trap within eight to ten years.'[1]

Most importantly, Kashf sees its role not only as one which can effectively alleviate poverty in Pakistan, but also one which is responsible for social and economic empowerment of women. By offering broader opportunities for impoverished women in the areas surrounding Lahore, Kashf believes that it can achieve its goals, which are:

> ...an increase in the income of working women and their family who make use of Kashf's credit and auxiliary services; an increase in assets over time as a consequence of an increased income stream and increased savings leading to all forms of increased assets; a diversification of income sources for loanees and earning members of the family; greater control over economic and social resources by the working poor, particularly women; an increase in decision-making capacity of women within households on account of the loans that they bring in and the increase in income that follows; enhanced leadership skills and bargaining capacity of women who interact with others when they form a group which allows them access to credit; an awareness of, and improvement in, social networking at the neighbourhood level; an improvement in inter-household gender relationships since it is they who actually bring in the loan; and an improvement in the financial management of household resources by borrowers and other beneficiaries.[2]

To those ambitious ends, Kashf has diversified its offerings to include products besides simple microfinance services, thereby expanding beyond a basic replication of Grameen's Group Lending Model. Such a broad spectrum of services is certainly commendable but is not available to the widest cross-section of eligible borrowers. We now turn to elements that directly affect outreach.

## WHO IS ELIGIBLE?

As per the Solidarity Group Lending Model, Kashf requires five women to form a peer group in order to obtain a loan. These groups are entirely self-selected, as in the Grameen system, and all five women must live in close geographical proximity to one another and must not be blood relations. In a notable deviation from Grameen's example, all borrowers must be married. The group then becomes the unit for all economic transactions conducted through Kashf, including loan appraisals, monitoring, enforcement of loan repayment and conflict resolution. Indeed, the group is intended to reinforce and promote behaviour according to Kashf's guidelines through peer monitoring, just as in Grameen.

Capacity building is an important aim of group formation: as groups are being formed, the loan officer will concentrate on training so that members understand what is being asked of them and become better equipped to manage their new resources and economic environment. During this time, members are encouraged to discuss their economic and entrepreneurial plans with one another.

Kashf believes that the exclusion of men is undesirable and may pose a hurdle in the proliferation of its efforts. As a result, Kashf creates a space for men during this consultation process. They are invited to attend meetings and observe programme conditions. Kashf specifically permits women to obtain loans on behalf of their husbands; hence both women clients and their male relatives are encouraged to participate in training sessions so that all parties are made aware of the requirements of the programme. This approach was designed to overcome possible objections to the economic activities and advancement of potential participants.

## INFRASTRUCTURE

Group leaders are elected by members, and five groups are arranged together to form a centre. Centre meetings then occur on a fortnightly basis during which the assigned loan officer meets at a predetermined home of one of the members to collect that term's repayment. Unlike the Grameen model, no area centres have been established: each centre selects a woman's house at which meetings will be held for the upcoming loan cycle. A centre manager and secretary are also selected and join the group leaders to form a credit committee responsible for all social and economic transactions in the centre.

Centres are then managed by an allocated branch which in turn is under supervision of an Area Office responsible for monitoring and collecting information from its designated area of jurisdiction. Social programmes are also organized by the Area Office, as also six-monthly plans and targets for the branches.

## SERVICES OFFERED

Kashf offers a variety of products for those who choose to participate in their programme, rather than affiliating themselves with the multitude of other microfinance schemes operating in the region. These products include:

**General Loan**: Initially only available in a standard amount of Rs 4000, the loan size is now more flexible and is determined by the borrower's capacity to repay and the profit potential of the business. It is repayable in twenty-two equal instalments over twelve months and can be renewed and increased annually. Renewal is contingent on both the group and the centre's ability to repay all their loans.

**Consumption Loan:** Given up to a maximum of Rs 300, this loan is intended to meet unforeseen emergencies and is repayable in twelve equal instalments over six months. The size of this loan was originally tied to the customer's savings: up to three times the amount saved could be borrowed. In 2001, the savings requirement was dropped.

**Emergency Loan:** Those who have joined Kashf to supplement their entrepreneurial activities are also eligible for the Emergency Loan, described by Kashf to be similar to a 'credit card for the poor'. Immediate and emergency consumption needs can be met by applying for the Rs 2000 loan which can be repaid over a period of six months (eleven instalments). Expenditure on account of utility bills, school books, clothing and health care can all be paid for by this loan.

**Savings:** A voluntary savings product is also offered by Kashf. Clients are able to deposit and withdraw at their leisure at centre meetings or at the branch office. While the Grameen model has compulsory savings accounts, Kashf has commoditized savings into an optional endeavour. Frugality and consciousness for the future are key components of the Grameen approach to savings; Kashf's approach, however, does not have the same emphasis.

**Life Insurance:** In case of death of either the client or the spouse, Kashf pays Rs 7500 to the deceased's family for expenses in addition to writing-off the loan. A premium of Rs 100 is levied on a loan of Rs 10,000 with an additional charge of Rs 10 for each Rs 1000 increase in the loan amount.

## APPROACH TO SOCIAL REFORM

Whereas Grameen relies on market influence and natural progression of social liberalization via financial freedom, Kashf institutes what it terms 'social intermediation services' along with its financial provisions. The Social Advocacy and Capacity Building Programme aims to strengthen community solidarity to build client trust in Kashf as well as to promote awareness of gender issues. Dialogue is promoted in scheduled training meetings in which women are encouraged to examine social myths and their own changing perceptions of themselves. Distinct programmes are offered within the Social Advocacy framework: leadership training which focuses on team building and conflict resolution; gender training in which both men and women discuss issues of sex, gender in society and domestic violence; and reproductive health education which give training in prenatal and post-natal care and addresses myths on contraception and sex issues. These programmes adopt a more planned and targeted approach to social reform than those of Grameen and as such require more financing as well.

## NOTES

1. Department for International Development, 'Kashf Evaluation Summary'. Department for International Development Paper Series, 2003.
2. Sarah Mosedale, *Case Study of Kashf Foundation*. Kashf Foundation (Lahore, 2002).

# CHAPTER THREE
# Grameen Model Evaluation and Assessment

Grameen's model is well-tailored to the environment in which it thrives: it takes into account the social relationships which govern village society as well as the social norms which constrict women's access to other financial means. That most financial transactions are conducted in the village is of note: this not only makes the Bank more accessible to village women but also helps to circumvent their exposure to the intimidating environment of a commercial bank. Taking into account the likelihood of intimidation, Grameen simplifies many of its rules not only to make them easily understood but also because transparency of its transactions helps to create trust. The primary group of five is small enough to make possible frequent contact amongst members and foster close personal relationships; centres with thirty to forty members have a more efficient size for conducting credit transactions but are large enough to create an identity within a community and give the individual member a sense of belonging to an organization.

Furthermore, weekly repayment allows borrowers to pay loan instalments from generated income rather than the original capital. As a result borrowers say they are able to accumulate capital soon after they join Grameen. Also shown in the study was that the borrower's capital base increases significantly as subsequent loans are taken, allowing for medium- and long-term investments in things such as machinery, cattle, tools and equipment. This investment pattern promotes the household's capacity to sustain gains over a long period of time. Moreover, accumulated investments and savings have proven to improve the ability of the poor to cope with natural disasters such as the 1998 floods in Bangladesh.[1]

The emphasis on self-initiative and self-employment rather than consumption also creates new employment insofar as it helps introduce women into the labour force. Thirty-one per cent borrowers reported that they were unemployed prior to joining Grameen claiming that they did not have the opportunity to work outside their own homes. Self-employment addresses many of the social issues that impact the ability to work: surveyed women answered that they were able to freely incorporate their entrepreneurial activities with their daily duties of child rearing and household management. For those who did have prior occupations beyond household duties, the average period of employment increased from about six working days to eighteen working days per month upon joining Grameen.[2] Naturally, income increase is also an outcome of increased employment: income in member households was 28 per cent higher than in non-participating households in Grameen villages. The higher incomes of Grameen households were attributed to increases in income from processing, manufacturing, trading and providing transport services—all financed with loans from Grameen Bank. Per capita food consumption also increased in member households as did investments in housing, education and sanitation.[3]

Though the emphasis of Grameen is not on consumption, a World Bank study found that 'profits from Grameen-financed businesses were increasing borrowers' consumption by 18 per cent per year, and that the percentage of Grameen borrowers living in extreme poverty was reduced by 70 per cent within 4.2 years of joining.'[4] A Grameen Bank internal survey reported that by 2001, 42 per cent of all member families had crossed the poverty line.[5] More than 91 per cent borrowers reported that Grameen had made a positive contribution to their standard of living.

The Sustainable Group Lending Model pioneered by Grameen is most fascinating when studied in the context of family units, not just individuals. That women are targeted by Grameen is the key: the Special Unit on Microfinance of the United Nations Capital Development Fund (UNCDF) reported that 'women's success benefits more than one person. Several institutions confirmed the well-documented fact that women are more likely than men to spend their profits on household and family needs. Assisting women therefore generates a multiplier effect that enlarges the impact of the institutions' activities.'[6] Naila Kabeer adds that it has been popularly demonstrated that 'women's interests are likely to be better served by investing effort and resources in the collective welfare of the household rather than in their own personal welfare.'[7] Proponents of targeting women cite women's repayment records as evidence of their benefit to institutional sustainability, reinforcing the collective wisdom that women's repayment rates surpass those of men.

But the Sustainable Group Lending Model does alienate some: the Grameen system capitalizes on the ability of women to pressure one another to repay loans. Social capital, so vital to life in a village, translates into the exclusion of women who doubt their own ability to make timely repayments and comply with the rules of Grameen Bank. Though this does protect Grameen from loan default, it also requires that potential borrowers should have prior confidence in their own abilities before approaching Grameen. In studying attrition rates in Grameen villages, Khandker concluded that factors which prevented many from joining in the first place were similar to those which led to drop-out after one cycle. These factors include lack of a reliable source of income and marriage to irresponsible men both of which result in a lack of income security to make weekly repayments. Borrowers in these situations were often forced through social pressures to leave their group.[8] In short, the effect of poverty is more than deprivation of financial opportunity: it may cultivate an environment which deprives many the ability to grasp opportunity at all. This poses a problem for the Grameen model's ability to reach the masses as there are simply too many people who cannot be reached through such means. However, as Grameen's mission is to help people 'help themselves', this situation does not challenge Grameen's *raison d'etre* or its claims.

Grameen's credit environment must be understood whilst analysing its success: as the pioneer of Solidarity Group Lending, Grameen did not face competition when entering the market for microfinance. That this notion was unheard of led to unique difficulties in establishing credibility, as Yunus elaborates in interviews. Women were initially distrustful of the system as its aim to provide credit to the non-creditworthy seemed contradictory. Men were opposed because of the possible social upheaval that might result from women generating their own independent income. To alleviate these concerns Yunus, and now Managing Director Nurjahan Begum, travelled to individual villages convincing people that the programme would be to their benefit. Accusations and suspicion regarding the programme abounded. Finally, Yunus and Nurjahan Begum managed to answer this criticism by establishing a small lending group whose success led to the spread of the idea.

The revolutionary concept of Grameen was introduced at a time of widespread destitution after debilitating famines had ravaged Bangladesh. The timing likely enhanced the reception of this unconventional approach: prevailing means of alleviating poverty were failing, and as such those who were suffering were more willing to try something to better their lives. Moreover, the inventive approach of Grameen benefited its growth which was advertised through publicity and by word of mouth.

Grameen's efforts have become widespread, and its current credit environment does face some competition. We will examine the importance of competition in later chapters. The Bangladesh Rural Action Committee (BRAC) is a major competitor of Grameen in many villages, with significant overlap in the target areas of both groups. By questioning villagers one learnt of instances of BRAC and Grameen functioning in the same villages. BRAC is more focused on capacity building than Grameen: BRAC's strategy therefore includes courses in human rights and legal education, provision of legal aid clinics, theatre as a means of raising awareness of social problems, household visits by volunteer health workers and gender equality training. Furthermore, BRAC's mission statement claims that it aims to reach the 'hard core poor' mentioned above, entailing a more aggressive, intensive approach than that of Grameen. That Grameen does not operate in urban areas also limits its target size. Grameen's niche in the credit market particularly targets self-motivated rural women who require capital to develop their entrepreneurial ability.

Finally, Grameen must be lauded for its extraordinarily strong institutional identity. That Grameen is a well-established chartered bank grants the institution more legitimacy than if it were to be simply another NGO. Also, conflict with the government has been minimal because while the government gives Grameen official support it provides no financial aid to the institution; were the support to extend to explicit financial donation, concerns about corruption could possibly emerge. The transparency of the organization at every level does lessen these concerns of corruption. Grameen's transparency, coupled with the cultivation of a strong identity and compelling vision, has been very important in generating support and guiding its staff in the field. Furthermore, it lends credibility to the Bank's functions, instilling the trust that is a prerequisite to participation in microfinance.

## NOTES

1. Saeed Qureshi, Ijaz Nabi and Rashid Faruqee, 'Rural Finance for Growth and Poverty Alleviation'. Policy Research Working Paper 1593 (World Bank, Agricultural and Natural Resources Division, 1996).
2. Grameen Informational Packet. Provided by Grameen Trust on 18 June 2005.
3. *Grameen Performance Summary, 2003*. Provided by Grameen Trust on 18 June 2005.
4. Irfan Aleem, 'Imperfect Information, Screening, and the Costs of Informal Lending: A Study of a Rural Credit Market in Pakistan'. *World Bank Economic Review* (Vol. 4, 1990).
5. *Grameen Performance Summary*, op. cit., 24.
6. Rani Deshpanda. 'Increasing Access and Benefits for Women: Practices and Innovations among Microfinance Institutions—Survey Results' (New York: UNCDF, 2001): 3.
7. Naila Kabeer, 'Money Can't Buy Me Love? Re-evaluating Gender, Credit and Empowerment in Rural Bangladesh'. Institute of Development Studies Discussion Paper 363 (Brighton, England: Institute of Development Studies, 1998).

8. Shahidur Khandker, Baqui Khalili and Zahed Khan, 'Grameen Bank: Performance and Sustainability'. World Bank Discussion Paper 306 (Washington, DC, 1995).

CHAPTER FOUR
# Kashf Model Evaluation and
Assessment

Poverty alleviation finance has precursors in Pakistan: the Agricultural Development Bank in the 1970s extended financial services to poor and low-income Pakistanis with support from international funding agencies. Rural support programmes, providing a host of social services, later took up the role of providing the poor access to financial services. Some rural support programmes developed specialized microfinance divisions, one of which would become Kashf. Pakistan received donor funding estimated at approximately US$400 million over the past five years; however, the Consultative Group to Assist the Poor (CGAP) in their April 2007 assessment reports that there is a lack of strong, sustainable institutions in Pakistan able to have a sincere impact on poverty in the nation.[1] With 10 million adults, considered eligible for microfinance services, Pakistan is one of the largest microfinance markets in the world. Only 600,000 adults actually receive these services, with Kashf serving 136,015 of them as of December 2006. The Pakistan Microfinance Network identifies Kashf as one of two self-sustaining microcredit institutions in the country: it is precisely because Kashf is sustainable and successful that it should serve as a prime example for other institutions in Pakistan. To reach high-growth demands, it is necessary to first examine the structure of Kashf, how it has tailored its services to its specific environment and what factors should be examined in order to achieve maximum market penetration.

Notably, Kashf employs a more cohesive approach to microfinance with an approach that incorporates education and training more so than Grameen's strict emphasis on entrepreneurship and self-initiative. Women in Pakistan, as in Bangladesh, have historically been poorer, less healthy and less educated than men, indicated by comparisons in the male and female Human Poverty Index (HPI).[2] Though the HPI does indicate that living standards in Pakistan decreased amongst both genders, the gap between the two increased from 9.5 index points in 1970 to 14.8 index points in 1995. Women suffered more drastically than men from the decrease in HPI, which is calculated through an analysis of education levels and opportunity, health care and living standards. These factors suffered a significant decline in the years prior to Kashf's establishment, as women bear a disproportionately large share of the burden of poverty. This results from limited access to economic opportunities and social services as well as restricted mobility, low social status and lack of ready access to productive assets such as land and agriculture. The manifold reasons for dire female poverty help to explain why Kashf targets factors more diverse than just access to financial services.

An analysis of Kashf's performance must take into account its credit environment and its competitors: Pakistan's rural credit market is marked by the coexistence of formal, semi-formal and informal lenders. The Agricultural Development Bank of Pakistan (ADBP) is the primary formal institution while NGOs participating in smaller microfinance and support operations constitute the semi-formal.[3] Aleem and Ghate report that formal and semi-formal financial institutions have historically covered a very small share of rural credit markets.[4] Qureshi, Nabi and Faruqee add that only 10 per cent of rural borrowing households in Pakistan borrowed from formal sources and less than 1 per cent from semi-formal sources.[5] Importantly, Kashf's model targets those who are unable to access formal sources and therefore must turn to informal sources.

The credit environment which Kashf entered was dominated by informal credit sources based on personal contacts and local access. Goheer reports that the informal market was divided into four categories:[6]

1. Social arrangements: Representing one-third of non-institutional credit, friends and relatives often do not charge interest and operate with assumed reciprocity. Availability is dependent on location and contacts.
2. Commercial arrangements: Often intermediated by commission agents or traders, this sort of credit is linked with the supply of input or purchase of output. This is also common among the rural poor. A high rate of interest is common, ranging from 10 to 25 per cent per month.
3. Land-based arrangements: Credit is extended by landlords to tenants and subsistence farmers for purchase of inputs and consumption. Though no collateral is required, rural credit surveys show that rates charged by landlords are about 60 per cent higher than institutional rates.
4. Moneylenders: This does not constitute an important source of informal credit as Islam considers usury an unworthy practice. There is great variation in interest rates.

Customers frequenting the aforementioned sources are often entirely shut out of the formal market; therefore Kashf's entry provides an opportunity for obtaining legitimate, consistent and formal credit without exorbitant interest rates. Kashf has also moulded itself to the specific demands in Pakistan as outlined by the Asian Development Bank (ADB), including: 'small and frequent loans; terms compatible with the nature of activity; preference of women due to restricted mobility; and significant and sustained social preparation to familiarize the poor with entrepreneurship.'[7] DFID, in their impact assessment of Kashf's microfinance programme in 2003, observed that the committee system used by Kashf (and pioneered by Grameen) may be the 'most effective form of savings and credit system' for the underdeveloped world.[8] Customer satisfaction is reported to be 94 per cent, with 75 per cent stating that without credit from Kashf business activities would have been impossible.[9] Sixty-three per cent clients said that credit was aimed at economic activities and notably 32 per cent client households moved across the poverty line in one year.

Though Kashf has been successful in helping those who join, it has not sufficiently penetrated the market. ADB suggests that non-financial constraints to microfinance outreach remain significant including 'barriers affecting women's access, vulnerability of the poor to economic and physical downturns, lack of skills for effective utilization of microfinance services, and inadequate access to basic infrastructure facilities.'[10] While it is true that Kashf's microfinance efforts have well-served its existing clients, microfinance in Pakistan has only penetrated less than 5 per cent of the 6.3 million poor households.[11]

## NOTES

1. H. Burki, *Microfinance Performance in Pakistan 1999-2005: Growth, but a Structural Flaw Persists*. Pakistan Microfinance Network, 2006.
2. Naila Kabeer, 'Agency, Well-being & Inequality: Reflections on the Gender Dimensions of Poverty'. (Sussex: Institute of Development Studies Bulletin 27, 1996): 11–21.
3. Nabeel Goheer, 'Microfinance: A Prescription for Poverty and Plight of Women in Rural Pakistan', Rural Finance for Growth and Poverty Alleviation. Available at: http://www.gdrc.org/icm/country/pak-microfinance.pdf
4. Aleem, op. cit., 46.

5. Qureshi, Saeed, Nabi, Ijaz and Faruqee, Rashidur R., 'Rural Finance for Growth and Poverty Alleviation (April 1996)'. World Bank Policy Research Working Paper No. 1593.
6. Nabeel Goheer, 'Microfinance: A Prescription for Poverty and Plight of Women in Rural Pakistan'. Rural Finance for Growth and Poverty Alleviation. Available at: http://www.gdrc.org/icm/country/pak-microfinance.pdf
7. Ashok Sharma, 'Developing Microfinance in Pakistan'. Asian Development Bank (Volume 2, Issue 4, 2001).
8. Department for International Development, 'Kashf Evaluation Summary'. Department for International Development Paper Series, 2003.
9. Roshaneh Zafar, 'Microfinance and women's empowerment: turning lead into gold?' *Development Bulletin* (57, February 2002): 63–6.
10. Ashok Sharma, 'Developing Microfinance in Pakistan'. Asian Development Bank (Volume 2, Issue 4, 2001).
11. Burki, op. cit., 56.

# CHAPTER FIVE
# Comparative Analysis of Results

The Grameen model and the Kashf adaptation model have key differences mainly because of the environment in which each was instituted. Kashf's purpose is diversified and goes beyond simple financial advancement due to the poverty index factors that existed prior to Kashf's inception; Grameen responded purely to the lack of finances and access to financial services faced by the poor in Bangladesh. Though environmental differences will be elaborated upon later, below are several of the key differences in the respective versions of the model:

## DESIGNATION OF LOAN

In the Grameen model, loans are strictly intended to promote income-generating activities so that loan repayment is assured. Promoting income generation also allows for an accumulation of capital as repayment is often taken from additional income made on a weekly basis. By contrast, loans from Kashf can also be used for supplementing consumption; only 63 per cent loans were actually used toward income generation. Kashf claims that this approach gives households greater flexibility and reduces their vulnerability to financial fluctuations.

## GENDERED ACCESS TO LOAN

Grameen makes provisions for lending to males: if men organize groups and centres following the same methodology as women, they are also eligible to borrow from Grameen. If a man is unable to find four other borrowers to join his group, he is simply unable to borrow from the institution. There is no flexibility in this regard.

Six per cent of Grameen clients are men organized in such groups. In this way, Grameen offers financial access to men rather than excluding them from financial opportunity. Kashf includes men in a different manner: men are told that they can receive loans through their female relatives. Women are explicitly allowed to borrow money on behalf of their husbands or for their businesses in direct contrast to Grameen's policies.

Although this practice also occurs in the Grameen model, it is not encouraged as it is believed it prevents women from taking control of their own financial destinies. Kashf on the other hand believes that allowing women to help their husbands with the loan increases their value in the household because they become a source of financial income. It is worth noting, however, that such a rule makes a woman particularly vulnerable in case of default. The Grameen model uses peer pressure to discourage this practice, effectively reducing its occurrence.

## STAGE IN WHICH LOAN IS RECEIVED

Participation in the Grameen programme is open to any woman who believes she is capable of managing a business. Kashf, however, restricts access only to married women. The rationale is that unmarried women are prone to moving out of a geographical location after marriage, and moving implicitly indicates loan default. But the exclusion of unmarried women prevents single women from developing enough capital and self-sufficiency prior to marriage that would allow them to enter the contract with a certain amount of economic bargaining power. Were Kashf to allow single women to participate, the system could work to empower women prior to their marriage: as observed in Grameen, participation in entrepreneurial activity enhances women's self-empowerment and initiative. Confidence and initiative in combination can positively benefit gender relations in marriage. The exclusion of single women inhibits free choice in group formation; if single women were actually too risky to be included into a group, then the group formation process would exclude them on basis of reputation.

## TRAINING VS. CREATIVITY

Kashf, realizing that a lack of confidence and resources can prevent successful entrepreneurship, offers training and a 'customer responsive approach based on understanding the market.' The latter is the largest deviation from the Grameen credit model as Grameen does not engage in 'social preparation', choosing instead to let one's own initiative guide entrepreneurship. Refraining from engaging in training significantly reduces Grameen's overhead cost and also allows women to self-develop their skills. Grameen's hands-off approach, however, makes little provision for difficulties encountered by women while embarking on income generation activities, for example, confusion regarding business opportunities or spousal objections. Kashf offers training and advice on how to address these obstacles.

## SAVINGS RATES

Kashf and Grameen have very different approaches to the savings aspect of the microfinance model. Grameen believes that mandatory savings builds up a safety net for possible future disasters; moreover, mandatory savings' programmes also encourage forethought and provide practise for future planning, both of which are conducive to promoting long-term investment and growth. Kashf on the other hand believes that its savings' programmes must allow customers flexible and free access to their own money.[1] Consequently subscription to its savings' programmes is entirely voluntary. Though the majority of Kashf borrowers do in fact save in some capacity, a set pattern of routine saving is not cultivated. Moreover, interviews conducted in Ravi Rayon indicated that women often save meagre amounts for very short periods but can access their saved funds with ease. Savings with Kashf greatly differ to Grameen's savings' programme in that Grameen rigidly demands financial discipline whereas Kashf leaves financial matters to the discretion of the borrower.

## INTEREST RATES

There is a significant difference in the interest rates charged by Kashf and Grameen, though both rates draw ire from clients. Kashf charges a 20 per cent flat interest; Grameen charges 20 per cent interest on a declining balance which averages to be approximately 10 per cent. Kashf's interest rate has been criticized by many as being extortionate but is explained as necessary to cover overhead cost. Regardless, criticism of Kashf's high interest rate is vocalized by the participants and general observers alike. Of the eighteen interviewees from Bedian centre, twelve identified high interest rate as a significant deterrent for prospective borrowers.

## ATTRITION RATE

Kashf's own 2001 report makes a note of its concern over the relatively high attrition rates from the programme. Branch level reviews indicate that much of the attrition results 'from client expulsion for poor performance rather than from them opting to leave'; the mechanism by which self-selection occurs in group formation must be examined in greater detail to reduce attrition. Better client screening could alleviate problems of client expulsion. Moreover, increased and intensive training prior to loan disbursal could also be useful. Other reasons to leave include: the heavy opportunity cost of meetings, insufficient size of loans and relocation from centre area. Grameen's reports do not demonstrate a similar concern over attrition rates.

## DISCIPLINARY ISSUES

Attendance at centre meetings seems to be more of an issue at Kashf than at Grameen. In response, Kashf has instituted certain policy changes to spur customer loyalty including relaxing the requirement of attending centre meetings.[2] Such a move, though addressing the concerns of clients, does diminish a key component of the success of the Grameen credit model: Grameen prides itself on the discipline instilled in its clients, reinforcing discipline through salutes, chants and repetition of the Sixteen Decisions. A lack of discipline in centre-meeting attendance could erode general discipline and not only have an adverse impact on repayment behaviour but also the overall attitude towards borrowing.

Chants, salutes and repetition of the Sixteen Decisions were also mentioned as methods which encouraged discipline and structure. Hashemi's findings also suggest that client discipline is reinforced by the structure of the meetings in which groups are arranged in lines with leaders at the head, and where all discussions are conducted in a similarly structured manner.[3] A strong group identity is created by this structure, and women are provided a public identity, an ability to organize and hold meetings, speak formally and carry out banking transactions in an orderly manner; all these contribute in cultivating a culture of discipline. This discipline translates into maintaining regular repayment schedules and efficient entrepreneurial management. Similar discipline-cultivating measures are not instituted at Kashf: the centres that were observed did not have a highly organized meeting pattern, and six of the eight centres observed suffered from an extreme lack of punctuality by its members.

## NOTES

1. Zafar, op. cit., 4.
2. Mosedale, op. cit., 6.
3. Syed M. Hashemi, 'Rural Credit Programs and Women's Empowerment in Bangladesh'. *World Development Journal* (Vol. 24, No. 4, 1996).

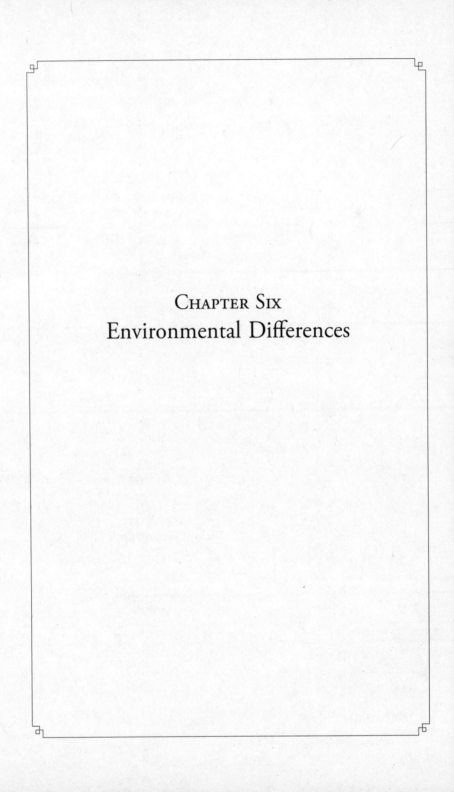

# CHAPTER SIX
# Environmental Differences

Bangladesh and Pakistan, although former halves of one nation, have environments that differ in many ways— a factor that might explain some of the differences in the successful assimilation of microfinance in these two countries. A study of both Kashf and Grameen revealed certain institutional differences which emerge as the most obvious factor for disparity in their respective success levels; however, by examining similarities in culture and environment and the resulting responses, one may get an insight into reasons why the success of Grameen could not be replicated in Pakistan with the same efficacy. The following includes an overview of potential factors for change and difference in outreach; they are intended to be topics for further research and investigation.

## Socio-political Factors

### Feudalism

Notably, the areas in which Kashf operates are still heavily influenced by feudal landlords. The existence of a feudal structure does not encourage individual entrepreneurship. Indeed, the long-standing feudal tradition, pseudo-feudal infrastructure and associated norms instead provoke suspicion of any individual self-sufficiency programme. The feudal system premises itself on organized subordination and hierarchy; any system designed to liberate individuals to obey only their own entrepreneurial impulses and thus gain financial independence is not conducive to feudal organization.

Bangladesh does not have such a strong tradition of feudalism and its people therefore do not face obstacles or intense, entrenched bias against individual motivation. Feudal hold over the distribution of income has historically prevented economic growth from trickling down to the masses; for example, though Pakistan enjoyed a high rate of GDP growth from 1960–1990, there was no reduction in poverty and instead the HDI suffered a further decline.[1] Furthermore, land-based credit is an important informal instrument of credit available to the poor, especially in Sindh, Balochistan and southern Punjab. As mentioned earlier, no collateral is required but the interest rate for this loan is approximately 60 per cent higher than institutional rates at any given time. The entry of an institution which encourages individual economic growth, self-empowerment and self-employment and at the same time denies landlords income derived from informal credit offerings would obviously not be welcomed by the feudals. To operate in an area dominated by feudal landlords is therefore extremely difficult: the opposition on this front is more pervasive and widespread than that faced by Bangladeshis in their pursuit of affordable credit. Negotiating with feudal lords for the introduction of microfinance seems futile; since economic self-sufficiency of the poor is not in the interests of these feudal lords, they pose a significant obstacle to microfinance institutions operating in their areas.

## Opposition Rooted in Cultural Interpretation of Religion

Grameen countered religious opposition soon after coming into being by engaging local religious leaders in the process: Muhammad Yunus documents how imams were addressed by Grameen officials in each village to make it perfectly clear that microfinance did not encourage acts that were contrary to the tenets of religion. Indeed, Grameen had to deal specifically with the issue of purdah that is widely practised in rural Bangladesh: women who observed purdah did not believe in ever leaving their homes, let alone interacting and being in close proximity to men in any social context.

Kashf's operating area in the Punjab has regions in which public activities of women are subject to a few restrictions, but these are not more preventive than the practice of purdah. Women interviewed in Ravi Rayan negotiate severely limited mobility, especially those who work as day labourers. The status of women is dissimilar from those rural Bangladeshi women who were prevented from work; rather, the Punjabi women interviewed were not as restricted from the public sphere as their Bangladeshi counterparts. This should mean lesser objection to women's involvement in entrepreneurial activities, so perhaps the cultural opposition to women's participation in the public sphere cannot so easily be identified as the reason for stifled growth.

In any case, the entrepreneurial activity of women does pose a challenge to traditional conceptions of the feminine role: the Solidarity Group Lending Model of Grameen does require its members to counter traditional patriarchal norms by assembling in public and interacting with men from outside the community. Receptivity to the disruption of these norms depends on the intensity of the desire to make economic gains: Grameen's growth flourished not only because Yunus and Nurjehan Begum engaged religious officials and convinced them of the merit of microcredit, but also because the economic situation was so dire that there was greater willingness to experiment with unconventional ideas. Deeply entrenched cultural beliefs can be expected to pose some sort of obstacle, but it is overly simplistic to attribute all obstacles to microcredit to these beliefs.

## Men's Role in Microcredit

Grameen began as a programme offering microcredit services to the poorest of the poor: initially this included impoverished men and women. Yet as the programme developed, it became clear that not only were women poorer than men in terms of assets and opportunity, but also that men were more likely to default on their loans and were, as such, less reliable risks. Though the majority of clients are now women, men still participate in Grameen as 6 per cent of the client base. Men are expected to follow the same rules as female participants in that they must find four other unrelated men to form a group and use that unit as a means of obtaining credit.

Recognizing that women in Pakistan are the poorest of the poor in terms of opportunity access, Kashf initially prepared a programme that was exclusively for women. After maintaining an all-female borrowing base until 2005, Kashf's borrowers are now 98.2 per cent female. ADB has specifically recognized that 'social intermediation costs to enhance women's access to microfinance are significantly higher in Pakistan': mobility constraints, cultural norms dictating social interaction and an absence of cohesive skills' development are major hurdles encountered in Pakistan and these are of a greater magnitude than those encountered in other countries, including Bangladesh.[2] A Pakistani approach to finance must then address those social intermediation costs as well as the male role in microcredit; exclusion of males from the process is not an option as a chauvinistic society will not tolerate a programme promoting financial independence of women on any other terms but its own.

Kashf's programme has attempted to incorporate men by allowing women to borrow loans for the enhancement of their husband's business but this may negate its goal of female development and empowerment which requires women to exercise their *own* financial initiative. Furthermore, this does not actually address those men who feel threatened by the notion of microcredit as a whole. Increased presence of women in the public sphere, made possible by their economic 'empowerment', translates into a challenge of male-dominated space.[3] This is especially true in contexts like Pakistan and Bangladesh, where market activities are largely seen as the domain of men.

Grameen's rhetoric praises women for their trustworthiness and capability in repayment, but also carries with it the implication that men are unreliable. This often translates to an exclusion of men, inciting retaliatory violence and other obstacles to smooth participation in microfinance institutions (MFI) activity. Kashf claims that by allowing women to borrow on behalf of men, the entire family unit can be strengthened because the process entails joint financial decision-making. Kashf claims that including men in the process would also have the affect of allaying fears of those men who are apprehensive of microfinance. Participation in microcredit programmes, especially those like Grameen and Kashf which require time commitments for weekly meetings and group collaboration, monopolizes time otherwise accorded to household labour, disrupting the 'social technology'.[4] Such trivial disruptions of household routine often cause intra-household conflict.[5] This works to the detriment of the double-bottom line of microcredit, which champions both women's empowerment and financial advancement.

## Economic Factors

### Bangladeshi Famine of 1974

Economic activity lagged in Bangladesh after the 1971 India-Pakistan war which resulted in its separation from Pakistan: a downward spiral of real income and rising unemployment continued as the task of rehabilitating returning refugees and recovering from disruption during the war took its toll. The living standard of the majority of the population would reach crisis levels by the end of 1973. To exacerbate this situation, Bangladesh experienced successive natural disasters together with international inflation, global food and oil crises, and poor administrative and economic management. The resultant famine was mainly a rural phenomenon, spurring the migration of thousands to cities and the deaths of hundreds of thousands who stayed back in the rural areas.

Yet the tragedy provided a perfect opportunity for establishing a new system of credit; confidence issues, though still pertinent, were possibly dismissed in light of an optimistic new process of self-sustenance. The presence of such dire poverty most likely created an opportunity for Grameen's success. Furthermore, a lack of confidence in new measures was in all probability obliterated because of the desperate desire for growth. Though Pakistan faced dire economic issues throughout the 1990s, it may be that Pakistan has not reached the critical point necessary for a rapid, widespread growth of opportunities provided to the poor by microcredit schemes.

### Government Presence and Economic Policy

Government intervention in creating a suitable environment in which microfinance can flourish is absolutely imperative.

Muhammad Yunus himself lauds the government support Grameen received and terms it as being instrumental in sustaining the institution's growth. The need for a microcredit wholesaler, says Yunus, is the most critical issue facing NGOs today: without one, long-term sustainability is precarious at best and NGOs will likely experience a 'virtual halt in their expansion programme, and find it difficult to continue their present programme because of lack of [consistent] funds.'[6] The interest rate policy of wholesale funds must therefore be carefully designed with a near-zero interest rate for start-up programmes and no more than the market rate for more mature programmes. This interest rate policy has been facilitating start-ups while maintaining sustainability by gradually offering market rates for the purchase of wholesale funds for distribution.

Both countries have commendably created microcredit wholesalers through governmental intervention. Bangladesh, with the cooperation of the World Bank, created a national wholesale fund called the Palli Karma-Sahayak Foundation (PKSF). This Foundation is responsible for making funds available to NGOs in order to spur growth rate and ensure consistent availability of funds. Approximately $262 million to nearly 200 NGOs has been distributed as funding for starting microcredit programmes and their subsequent expansion. Upon creation, the PKSF was kept independent from government influence and control to prevent the funds from becoming vulnerable to political tumult and turmoil. In Pakistan, the Pakistan Poverty Alleviation Fund has fashioned itself as a distributor of funds to microfinance groups looking for start-up capital, and is thereby encouraging the expansion of microfinance institutions in the country. Pakistan is therefore well funded with capital for expansion of microcredit services.

## INSTITUTIONAL FACTORS

### Strong Leadership

Yunus commands much respect from the clientele and indeed the population at large: he is seen as a charismatic, conscientious, humble leader with a simple approach to helping the poor. This image has helped him maintain a favourable political environment for microcredit. Furthermore, Yunus's efforts in the field and his hands-on approach have earned him the trust of many prospective clients, who view him as a caring father-figure rather than a distant head of a financial organization. This helps to enhance both transparency and accessibility. Participants in Grameen villages were able to easily name him as the founder of the institution; comparatively, women in Kashf programmes were not able to do the same for the leadership of that institution, indicating perhaps a detachment between the clients and the management. The lack of a close sense of identification with the institution may reduce trust and even accountability. Transparency and accessibility are two major components for creating the sort of trust needed for the healthy management and growth of microfinance endeavours because they allay suspicions and fears of exploitation and corruption.

### Emphasis on Disciplined Organizational Style

As discussed earlier, Grameen maintains an operating style focussed on disciplined behaviour. The operating style of Grameen is further characterized by austerity and a 'lack of frills' for the entire organization: the institution not only advocates frugal living, and within one's means, to ensure future financial stability, but itself follows this advice and leads by example. Field staff is encouraged to dress and live simply, and walk from village to village to demonstrate their humility and accessibility to clients. Yunus conducts his business in a modest office in a building which is not air-conditioned. Such small details reflect an orderly style of operating which dispel fears of corruption or exploitation.

A Kashf loan officer in Yakki Gate explained that a relaxed, comfortable operating style is in place in order to diminish intimidation associated with financial institutions. That Kashf chooses a more comfortable operating style is not inherently undesirable but it does little to make itself freely accessible to those who participate. As a result of exploitation by informal credit sources detailed earlier, clients are already wary of moneylending institutions; perhaps an added effort to encourage transparency and address these fears would benefit Kashf's image amongst potential clients. Kashf is excellent in selecting its loan officers, and by recruiting women who belong to the locality it earns them the trust of many prospective clients; however, it could be beneficial for Kashf if a similar selection criteria were applied throughout the organizational hierarchy.

## NGO or Bank?

Until very recently, Kashf existed as an NGO and not a financial institution: this designation prevented it from directly accumulating funds from clients. Instead, Kashf would collect funds and then the loan officer, centre leader and centre secretary would travel to deposit it in a bank. NGOs are unable to take public deposits because as per law they are not defined as financial institutions. The transformation of an NGO into a microfinance bank allows money to be mobilized to its full extent and permits self-reliance. Kashf's transition from an NGO into a microfinance bank should lower overhead costs, make it more effective and perhaps result in a decreased interest rate on loans to reflect its increased efficiency.

## Product Diversity

A diverse array of products offered to clients may comprehensively address all needs of the poor but the development of these products may detract from resources needed for market penetration. 'Inadequate specialization' is quoted by the ADB to be a common barrier to sustainability of microfinance operations of NGOs.[7] Methods of enhancing product diversity and outreach will be covered in detail in a later chapter.

Product diversity depends on the resource availability of a given microcredit institution. For those institutions operating on paltry budgets, product diversity may be elusive, particularly when simultaneously funding social initiatives. Combining social services with credit diverts funds that could otherwise be used for possible funding of outreach initiatives. Qureshi, Nabi and Faruqee (1996) demonstrated that the social engagement approach, though commendable, makes the mandate of such microfinance efforts too broad. Balancing both outreach and social services is financially unsustainable for many: the Qureshi study quotes the Comilla Cooperative Model of Bangladesh as an example, which faced 'serious repayment and viability problems' when its social service-oriented microcredit programme was replicated nationwide.[8] Other NGOs in Pakistan, such as the Aga Khan Rural Support Programme and the National Rural Support

Programme, have tried to address deficiencies in outreach through social services, but have met with only limited success.[9]

Regardless, Kashf maintains its diversified social services such as training programmes. Though social services may hinder outreach funding, it is important to realize that some form of risk aversion service may be necessary as a precursor to outreach. Poor households are likely to forego potentially viable technologies, production choices, and income opportunities due to risk aversion. Services and training aimed at risk aversion may actually be helpful in subverting these prohibitive attitudes, and therefore aid in outreach and expansion of services.

## High Interest Rate

Sensitivity to interest is particularly important in understanding possible aversion to joining microcredit programmes. Though it is difficult to redress distaste for interest that stems from religious beliefs, it is quite possible to address the issue of high rates charged by institutions because that is directly determined by them. Higher interest rates increase the apprehension associated with becoming indebted due to failed enterprises, and may be exacerbated because of prior experiences with unfair and exploitative informal lending sources.[10] A sustainable credit delivery system must balance its own overhead costs and costs of risk with availability and affordability to the clients; the rate must remain at a level low enough to be accessible but high enough to ensure sustainability.

Grameen maintains that its policy is to keep the interest rate as close as possible to the rate in the commercial banking sector. The market rate is taken as the reference and not the moneylender's rate. Kashf, which maintains a much higher interest rate on its loans, states that the higher rate is necessitated to offset additional operational costs resulting from its status of being an NGO.

Though high operating costs are understandable, a higher interest rate can draw criticism and even turn potential clients averse to participation. In the NWFP, for example, practitioners of microfinance have discovered that almost half the population is averse to taking loans on fixed interest: NGOs have been criticized and attacked for perpetuating a perceived 'non-Islamic' practice, and as such resentment against development institutions has grown immensely. The grounds for opposition have been that charging such interest has been exploitative: high interest rates, such as those charged by Kashf, are easily prone to that charge. This may be a barrier to Kashf's expansion of its services: poverty cannot be eliminated if the process is seen as threatening a tenet of faith.

## Gender Training

In patriarchal societies such as those seen in rural Bangladesh and rural and peri-urban Pakistan, the need for gender training would seem obvious: women participating in entrepreneurial endeavours will likely encounter men in contexts not quite usual for them. Inadequate social preparation can disrupt group cohesion and ultimately the sustainability of microfinance operations, so simply focusing the gender orientation of organizations towards women may not be sufficient.

Kashf provides gender sensitivity training so that men and women are encouraged to critically examine their approach to social roles. Even though this is commendable, the DFID examination of Kashf demonstrated that over 71 per cent participants in such trainings could not recall what was taught to them just two months later.[11] This indicates that perhaps the gender sensitivity approach is not effective in dispersing information. Additionally, conducting this training expends funds that could be more usefully allocated to other products and programmes. Grameen's approach is minimalist and does not offer any training or technical assistance relying instead on the ability, innovation and expertise of individuals to deal with their particular situations. Difficulties that arise are dealt with at the group and centre level with the guidance of the centre manager and the assistance of peers but otherwise there is no formal mechanism in place to specifically deal with these issues. This reduces overhead costs and allows for problems to be addressed at a local, more intimate and personal level.

### Savings Programme

Interestingly, Grameen Bank's approach to savings has been widely criticized by many, including participants and academics, for imposing strict restrictions on withdrawal of savings. Though members are able to open individual accounts to which they have easy access, most members' savings are in the form of group funds which are built up through a mandatory weekly deposit of a minimum of 2 takas per week; this amount can be increased to 10 takas per week, subject to a determination by the centre manager. These funds can be used by the group to make interest-free loans to members or alleviate pressures in case of emergencies such as health crises or business difficulties. Critics say that 'such restrictions have the unintended effect of discouraging savings, and thereby fail to take advantage of the substantial unmet need for savings facilities among the poor.' This resulted in a revamp of the system: savings can now be withdrawn by individuals with accumulated interest (8.5 per cent) after ten years. This modification still encourages a patient view of group savings and a focus on the future.

Grameen's rationale for mandatory group savings is to enable members to have a contingency plan in order to overcome crises they may encounter in the natural course of events. Women are susceptible to pressure from their families, and were they able to make individual withdrawals at whim, it would become difficult for them to maintain a high level of savings that could be effectively helpful in a serious crisis. A pooled savings' system also works to draw groups together: the prospect of losing one's savings discourages group attrition on account of trivial conflicts.

Kashf's savings' system differs quite extensively and allows frequent individual withdrawals. As such it does not provide the same sort of binding that a pooled savings' system does and could thus contribute to a lessened aversion towards attrition. Furthermore, savings are hard to maintain in this manner. There is no mechanism to ensure long-term savings, and observations and interviews revealed that savings were often depleted around Eid and during wedding celebrations. Accumulated savings help change the approach of poor women to money as well as encourage long-term planning and discipline. Kashf would be able to benefit from the development of such a programme, and in doing so could strengthen group bonds and reduce attrition rates of clients. It may be that Kashf does not mandate savings because it is an NGO and is thus unable to actually hold the savings' accounts; it can only hold and manage the savings if it is an actual bank. Upon becoming a bank, it might be that Kashf would encourage mandatory savings.

## Loan Officers

The gender of loan officers (LO) can affect the level of female participation in some social situations. Female LOs are necessary in strictly traditional areas where restrictions on interaction with an unrelated male would exclude many from participation. But in areas where enlisting female loan officers is considered more desirable, there is the possibility of not finding sufficient number of qualified women either because many candidates lack the requisite education or because they are reluctant to join due to safety concerns (i.e. for evening visits and travel). Despite the requirements of traditional rural environments, less than one-third of Grameen's field workers are female.

Observations have shown that women are more disciplined when administered by a male LO. Perhaps this can be attributed to the cultural view that men are more familiar with and more able to perform financial transactions, and as such respect accorded to their statements and orders is greater than that given to women who tend to be viewed more as peers than leaders. Kashf maintains that women readily identify themselves with female LOs because the latter engage them at a more personal level; this is why the majority of LOs employed by Kashf are females. Further research is necessary to determine what is more suited to the Pakistani environment.

# NOTES

1. Burki, op. cit., 15.
2. Sharma, op. cit., 57.
3. Kabeer, op. cit., 19.
4. Pierre Bourdieu, *The Logic of Practice* (Cornwall: Polity Press, 1990):119.
5. Muhammad Yunus, 'Expanding Microcredit Outreach to Reach the Millenium Development Goals'. Presented at the International Seminar on Attacking Poverty with Microcredit. Dhaka, Bangladesh. 9 January 2003.
6. Ibid.
7. Sharma, op. cit.
8. Saeed Qureshi, Ijaz Nabi and Rashid Faruqee, 'Rural Finance for Growth and Poverty Alleviation'. Policy Research Working Paper 1593 (World Bank, Agricultural and Natural Resources Division, 1996).
9. Sharma, op. cit., 23.
10. Grameen Informational Packet. Provided by Grameen Trust on 18 June 2005.
11. Mosedale, op. cit., 18.

# CHAPTER SEVEN
# On Empowerment

Much of microcredit's international acclaim is because of its success according to a 'double bottom line': that is, microcredit's purported ability to deliver economic advancement as well as improvements in gender equity.[1] The importance of the double bottom line is due to the feminization of poverty. A World Bank report illuminates this phenomenon, concluding that societies in which gender discrimination is institutionalized suffer from greater incidences of poverty, slower economic growth, weaker governance and a lower living standard.[2] The United Nations Development Programme (UNDP) reports a strong correlation between gender empowerment measures, gender-related development indices and the HDI. Furthermore, the UNDP reports that 70 per cent of the 1.3 billion people living on less than $1 a day are women.[3] A focus on women's advancement in society thus does not necessarily arise from a perspective of inherent equality, but from a concern with the sustained growth of the society at large. Both Grameen and Kashf cater almost exclusively to women, in recognition of the disproportionate representation of women among the world's poorest people. Both, as many microcredit providers tend to do, espouse a dedication to women's empowerment.

Comprehensive, integrated definitions of empowerment, however, are elusive. Interestingly, gender improvements championed as part of the 'double bottom line' are articulated as 'empowerment', despite a lack of an agreed-upon definition. It is essential to understand what exactly is meant by empowerment, and subsequently how this idea translates to implementing human development.

The development theory has very recently been transformed as a result of Amartya Sen's capability approach. Sen defines capabilities as freedoms, or the real opportunities of individuals to lead the lives they value.[4] At the crux of this conception is the issue of choice: that is, the ultimate objective of development is to facilitate freedom. Discourse on women's empowerment has been significantly influenced by this ideal. Developments in women's status have had the best results from those changes directly influencing the ability of women to exercise agency, including formal schooling and participation in the labour force. As a result, over time, the stated goal of women's empowerment evolved, from concentrating on the well-being of women in relation to their male counterparts to an emphasis on women's agency. Sen argues that women's agency, defined as a woman's ability to pursue her own valued goals, is the pathway of social change that holds the most potential for altering the lives of the impoverished.

The capability approach should be seen as a mode of thinking rather than a fixed formula: Sen's framework purposefully refrains from specificity in order to facilitate the very sense of autonomy and choice he proposes. Microcredit participation is championed as one method of increasing choice and capabilities: access to credit is thought to liberate women, enabling them to enter the labour force and pursue the entrepreneurial creativity stifled due to poverty. In short, entrepreneurship is thought of as freedom. Importantly, participation in a microcredit programme is thought to provide opportunities for women to engage in activities that help them to develop their 'self'.

Two pertinent theories speak directly to this enhancement or realization of a woman's sense of self: Bandura's concept of self-efficacy and Antonovsky's concept of a sense of coherence. To acquire skills such as financial management or income-generation capability increases a woman's belief in her ability to produce an intended and desired effect.[5] As Bandura elaborates, those equipped with a heightened sense of self-efficacy approach challenges from an empowered perspective, set higher goals and are committed to attaining these goals. Self-efficacy increases healthier behaviour and perpetuates through reinforcement the idea of agency and autonomy. Self-efficacy influences the production channel in this way. Antonovsky's conception of coherence pertains to a woman's three-part global concept: that is, comprehensibility, or the extent to which a woman can cognitively make sense of her external environment; manageability, or the extent to which a woman perceives that her available resources can be used to control the demands of her environment; and three, meaningfulness, the extent to which a woman's life makes emotional sense.[6] This idea of coherence is enhanced with access to entrepreneurship-enhancing credit. In short, it allows her to actualize her goals, which in turn speak to the coherent value of her efforts in directing her life. As a result of this enhanced sense of 'self', possible through self-efficacy and coherent life direction, entrepreneurship leads to empowerment.

These general theories of strengthening one's sense of 'self' are manifested in a variety of dimensions. These dimensions include material, cognitive, perceptual and relational pathways of positive change.[7] Material empowerment occurs through the expansion in the material resource base of women: this is clearly possible through mere access to credit, regardless of subsidiary or supplementary programmes. Cognitive empowerment occurs from a woman's recognition of her own abilities and skills. Through the enactment of a successful entrepreneurial venture, this cognitive faith in one's abilities is possible; however, unsuccessful ventures may be detrimental. A prioritization of this empowerment may lead an institution to value career training and business support. Perceptual empowerment occurs through changes in how others perceive the individual, indicated by a rise in social prestige. Often, this requires a positive view of participation in entrepreneurial activity, which may be difficult in areas where women have restricted mobility. Where entrepreneurship for women is frowned upon, perceptual empowerment may not be possible without large-scale shift in social perception of the status of women in the labour force. Consequently, institutions focused on perceptual status empowerment will initiate activity to convince social groups of the advantages in mobilizing women's financial capabilities. Finally, relational empowerment occurs in transformations within micro-level gender relations within the family. This is indicated by a specific reduction in gender inequality in social relationships. Microfinance initiatives concentrating upon alleviation of household gender equality might prioritize gender trainings and specific outreach relating to household management of capital.

These different approaches to empowerment can be collapsed into Mayoux's delineation of three paradigms of actualizing empowerment. All conceptualize access to financial services as 'reinforcing virtuous spirals' of increasing economic, social, political, and legal empowerment for women.[8] These paradigms prioritize empowerment in different ways. Importantly, they promote precise definitions of empowerment mechanisms. All have relatively consistent internal logic with respect to their translation into policies. Disagreement among them results from differing perspectives of key actors in the microcredit deployment. Staff involved in microfinance are often firm followers of the financial self-sustainability model, which prizes economic efficiency and sustainable practices as a means of promoting continued outreach and growth. Staff concerned with human development often have more sympathy for the poverty alleviation paradigm, championing participation and integrated development focused on social development as a key result of economic growth. Finally, those concerned with gender equity and women's rights look at the feminist empowerment paradigm, concentrating on microcredit's capacity for improving the status of women in developing countries as a priority result in development.

Under the financial self-sustainability model, programmes emphasize access to minimalist, economically sustainable microcredit institutions. This tends to attract those with established entrepreneurial ability who merely need credit to actualize their talents on a profitable scale. This model may also appeal to existing micro-entrepreneurs who require additional credit to scale-up their initiatives. In effect, this model targets the bankable poor, including small entrepreneurs and farmers, instead of attempting to reach all impoverished individuals. Women are selected as prime candidates for proponents of this model because of their higher repayment rates, a factor that facilitates financial self-sustainability for any institution. This paradigm underlies the microcredit models promoted by most donor agencies and the Best Practice guidelines delineated by USAID, World Bank, UNDP, and CGAP. Ultimately, the goal is to institute large, self-supporting programmes that can selectively reach out to the poor in the context of declining aid budgets, and opposition to welfare and redistribution in macroeconomic policies.

Here, accepting microfinance services is framed as an inherently empowering act: participation implicitly recognizes a mobilization against institutional barriers preventing the truly destitute from any semblance of self-sufficiency. As Baden and Milward explain, though 'women are not always poorer than men, the weaker basis of their entitlements [makes them] generally more vulnerable...and once poor, [women] have fewer options in terms of escape.'[9] Access to financial services which allow income generation expand the options for 'escape' from poverty; with the option of microfinance as a tool for generating income, women should theoretically be no longer economically dependent on others. This reduction in vulnerability provides a platform for self-empowerment should a woman decide to make that choice. Decision-making, resource-utilization and negotiating skills acquired by participating in a microfinance programme result in agency. Though many women participating in microfinance programmes have previously been denied this sense of agency, engagement with microfinance institutions theoretically necessitates the exercise of agency because that is inherent to entrepreneurship. Resources are allocated according to the wishes of the women involved and may be seen as inherently empowering because it requires the exercise of some sense of agency. Furthermore, financial security should provide women the freedom to express this agency without fear of economic repercussions. In sum, economic empowerment leads to improved well-being; social, political, and legal empowerment should follow shortly thereafter, despite a lack of explicit attention to other dimensions of gender subordination.

In the poverty alleviation model, attention is paid to the multifaceted causes of poverty, including the deep-rooted connection between patriarchy, power, and conflict.[10]

Microfinance should be part of an integrated community development plan. This mode of development will necessarily alleviate household poverty and thus propel community collective action. To incorporate the marginalized into community action, the poorest members of society are designated the target group of this particular model. Consequently, the rationale for targeting women is because they are often the poorest, and because they are most likely to spend income on the well-being of their impoverished families.

This model conceptualizes women's empowerment as the gateway to large-scale social empowerment for all. It sees women's improved credit access as a means of leveraging power in unequal gender relationships in the household. Because of this greater access, women are able to negotiate a better bargaining position. As a result, groups functioning under the poverty alleviation model may be more amenable to male use of a woman's loans, provided that it is geared towards family improvement. The model does not conclude, as the financial self-sustainability model does, that participation in a microfinance programme is sufficient for stimulating empowerment. In this model, it is thought that the coupling of financial services with proactive social development initiatives both stimulate self-empowerment of women in terms of agency as well as encourage better financial performance.

Dunford's research demonstrates that financial services coupled with social development initiatives such as education can allow for the creation of 'economies of scope' by 'packaging two or more services together to minimize delivery and management support costs [as well as] maximizing the variety of benefits for people's multiple needs and wants.'[11] Encouraging education and literacy training, for example, reinforces the self-motivation and curiosity necessary for success in an entrepreneurial environment. Discussion and support groups also facilitate improvement in business endeavours and provide the strong social network needed by women in an otherwise paternalistic and patriarchal society. Development of leadership attributes contribute to the aim of empowering women by raising their ability to assert themselves in environments where they were once discouraged to do so. This economic empowerment conceptualizes women's empowerment as a tool to alleviate whole-scale poverty.

Similarly, the feminist empowerment model also identifies women's empowerment as a development goal; however, it does not conceive it as beneficial because of its instrumentality, but rather intrinsically a development good in itself. Programmes emphasizing the feminist empowerment model will employ microcredit as part of sectoral strategies of women workers. In this way, the feminist empowerment model is concerned with equity in the larger social structure more so than the household emphasis delineated in the poverty alleviation model. The target group is of course women, but it also looks to incorporating men to achieve the rationale of actualizing equity and the human rights of women. The ultimate goal is the transformation of power relations throughout society, propelled by the underlying assumption that women must aim for social and political change in ways advocated by the international women's movement. Importantly, the feminist empowerment paradigm must not be seen as a Western/Northern imposition: it is firmly rooted in the development of some of the earliest Southern microcredit programmes.[12] This empowerment informs the gender policies of many NGOs. As a result, these NGOs will implement similar supplemental programmes that those functioning under the poverty alleviation model do, but for different motivations. Moreover, this may be coupled with larger lobbying initiatives.

That these models all envision different destinations for empowerment is apparent. As a result, the indicators demonstrating progress towards these destinations differ as well. Institutions may embody different models at diverse stages of their development.

Grameen, for instance, achieved wide outreach through a promotion of the financial self-sustainability model, allowing it to eventually diversify its offerings into a variety of industries dedicated to structural economic change. In terms of procedural empowerment, Grameen employs only the Sixteen Decisions, compressing factors of general female empowerment into a relatively static list to be obeyed. In this way, Grameen can be seen as a financial self-sustainability model that ultimately appropriated some concerns of the poverty alleviation model.

Kashf, by contrast, espouses the poverty alleviation model, with some elements of the feminist empowerment model. Kashf envisions empowerment involving change within the household, within the community, and at a broader institutional or policy-making level.[13] To achieve these goals, Kashf employs three indicators: the ability of the programme to generate enhanced trust, solidarity and social interaction; the impact of microcredit on women's self-confidence and self-esteem; and the opportunities created by the programme for leveraging and networking. This is a more hands-on approach for assessing empowerment than the position taken by Grameen. Moreover, these are examples of differing indicators that source from the model or models of empowerment prioritized by institutions.

Critiques of these indicators stem from inter-model incompatibilities or divergences in priority. For example, Pitt and Khandker identify empowerment as increased income resulting from increased earning time spent in credit-based activities.[14] A failure to see significant income increase would indicate, in this model, a failure to achieve empowerment; however, this indicator may elide the fact that household bargaining may have improved, or that the client has engaged in lobbying or agitation for women's rights in another, non-economic realm.

Goetz and Sen Gupta have perhaps one of the most famous critiques of microcredit's capacity for encouraging empowerment:[15] They measures a loanee's knowledge of issues related to her loan use ('managerial control') as an indication of her empowerment. This embodies an approach entrenched in the logic of the financial self-sustainability programme: financial knowledge indicators and proficiency in market access are seen as indicators of general empowerment. As above, this method of assessment excludes any understanding of household interactions or increased decision-making in other social capacities. This is sourced in the logic of the poverty alleviation model, which prioritizes household participation.

Others, steeped in the financial self-sustainability model, critique the feminist empowerment and poverty alleviation models for their wastefulness. Dunford, for example, elaborates upon the common fear that soft services such as literacy training, health education, business training and support groups are costly and often lack positive outcomes.[16] Moreover, empowering elements in MFI programmes may limit access to funds from bilateral and multilateral donor agencies, as most agencies' funding criteria focus on outreach rather than an ambiguous and difficult-to-measure social impact on clients. Empowerment-oriented programmes may also take away from financial sustainability ratios because valuable funds are then diverted from outreach and market penetration efforts; empowering programmes become designated as luxuries rather than a key element of programme design and goals. Ultimately, proponents of the financial self-sustainability model critique expensive programmes for detracting from outreach, pre-empting the very participation that is thought to translate into empowerment.

Those championing a promotion of women's agency through the feminist empowerment model may critique systems in which women may be obtaining loans on behalf of their husbands. This is seen as betraying a goal of enhanced, individual economic agency. Villages where women exercise less control over loan-funded enterprises tend to be located in more economically depressed areas where competition for economic resources is highly intense. In situations where such scarcity exists, men are more likely to appropriate women's loans and use them for their own means. Interestingly, however, this may result in an improvement in the household's overall health. Moreover, Hashemi suggests that women with little or no control over their own loans still have more empowerment than non-members: 'credit programme members who were contributing to family support were more likely to be empowered than those who were not contributing; however, members who were not contributing were more empowered than non-members.'[17] This suggests that some enhanced sense of agency is potentially available to those women who merely provide access to capital for their husbands, even though those rooted within the feminist empowerment model would consider this to be a failure.

The array of literature flatly rejecting the notion of empowerment through microcredit often argues that such programmes subject women to new paradigms of power subjugation. These critiques, however, stem from inter-model comparisons. All, however, define the absence of empowerment as the absence of operational choice: these critiques reference an oppressive nature perpetuated, established or reinforced by microcredit. Oppression of choice and empowerment are oppositional dialectics: therefore, the structures that best facilitate empowerment are those which facilitate the greatest breadth of choice.

Moreover, empowerment occurs through myriad processes, with many dimensions, and arrives at different materializations. The paths taken by respective institutions will reflect this diversity in underpinnings, methodology and indicators. Homogeneity of approach will elide the diverse circumstances in which empowerment is needed. Conceptualizing the microcredit-providing institution as an intervening force bestowing empowerment will inevitably fail: no definition of empowerment it puts forth will be sufficiently, comprehensively applicable. Empowerment can only be meaningful if it speaks to the specificities of women's preferences and life circumstances. Contextual variations and individual differences, combined with complex approaches to empowerment, necessitate an idea of empowerment as choice freedom. Ultimately, then, the MFI's role is to equip women to actualize their own definitions of empowerment: in this way empowerment remains a subjective value. The definition of empowerment is to be determined by the communities and individuals who seek it: it must not be a top-down, dictated outcome.

Women's voices and demands must be included. It is only with this priority that the pertinent, relevant empowerment-oriented actions can be actualized. In this way, capabilities theory translates to the ability of women to select a model of empowerment most relevant to their lifestyle and priorities. Participatory impact assessments work to this end. In simple language, this entails asking women whether their lives have improved through the services provided by the institutions of which they are clients. This is a responsive methodology of empowerment. Statistical findings can shed light on the magnitude of impact. Encouraging participants to voice their experiences allows for sincere insight into the performance of an MFI, rather than theorization of gender subordination or poverty alleviation. Independent assessments of client satisfaction and lived experience should necessarily involve testimony and contextual evidence rather than piecemeal proxy indicators attempting to satisfy pre-established hypotheses.

Institutions will naturally have varying interpretations of these needs, and different capacities with which to fulfil them. As seen above, institutions also embody distinct views of empowerment which will imbue their respective approaches to development. To achieve empowerment, then, a spectrum of distinctly-oriented institutions must be made available to women. This translates as a microfinance industry characterized by diversified, tailored offerings from MFIs, or even increased replications with intimate familiarity of discrete operating areas. In the next section, we will explore the role of trust in creating space for these new, varied institutions.

## NOTES

1. Linda Mayoux, 'Women's Empowerment Through Sustainable Microfinance'. Working Draft, September 2005.
2. World Bank, *Engendering Development: Through Gender Equality in Rights, Resources, and Voice* (Washington, D.C.: World Bank, 2001).
3. United Nations Development Fund for Women, 'Progress of the World's Women' (New York: United Nations Publications Series, 2000).
4. Amartya Sen, *Development as Freedom* (Oxford University Press, New Delhi, 1999).
5. Albert Bandura, 'Self-efficacy: toward a unifying theory of behavioural change', *Psychological Review*, 84(2), 1977: 191–215.
6. Aaron Antonovsky, *Unravelling the Mystery of Health. How People Manage Stress and Stay Well* (San Francisco: Jossey-Bass Publishers, 1987).
7. M.A. Chen, *Beyond Credit: A Subsector Approach to Promoting Women's Enterprises* (Canada: Aga Khan Foundation, 1996).
8. Mayoux, op. cit., 19.
9. Sally Baden and K. Milward, 'Gender and Poverty'. *Bridge Report* (Sussex: Institute of Development Studies, 1995): 30.
10. Ibid.
11. Chris Dunford, 'Building Better Lives: Sustainable Integration of Microfinance with Education in Health, Family Planning and HIV/ AIDS Prevention for the Poorest Entrepreneurs' (Washington, D.C.: Microcredit Summit Campaign, 2001): 2.
12. Katharine Rankin, 'Social Capital, Microfinance and the Politics of Development', *Feminist Economics* (Vol. 8 No. 1, 2002).
13. Department for International Development, op. cit.
14. Pitt and Khandker, op. cit.

15. A.M. Goetz and R. Sen Gupta, 'Who Takes The Credit? Gender, Power and Control over Loan Use in Rural Credit Programmes in Bangladesh', *World Development Journal* (January 1996).
16. Chris Dunford, op. cit., 2.
17. Syed M. Hashemi, 'Those Left Behind: A Note on Targeting the Hardcore Poor' in Geoffrey Wood and Iffath Sharif (ed.), *Who Needs Credit? Poverty and Finance in Bangladesh* (Dhaka: University Press Ltd, 1997).

# CHAPTER EIGHT
## On Trust as Enabling Empowerment

Empowerment stems from participation with institutions that enable the realization of choice-making freedom in various ways. To participate with such institutions, however, clients must first trust the institution's ability to actualize their goals of empowerment. In short, trust is a prerequisite for any participation.

Trust is both an outcome and an antecedent of relationships: it allows initial participation, perpetuates a functioning relationship and ultimately generates social capital. Bradach and Eccles define trust as a 'type of expectation that alleviates the fear that one's exchange partner will act opportunistically.'[1] It is both a type of behaviour[2] and an underlying disposition.[3] Trust is warranted when an individual expects benefit from making oneself vulnerable to another agent.[4] Moreover, Deutsch expands trusting behaviour to consist of acting despite the presence of a situation in which the penalty one suffers if the other abuses that vulnerability is greater than the benefit.[5] Through the trust calculus, the individual participates despite uncertainty regarding a future action of another individual or institution to affect her choice of action before she can monitor that action.[6] According to Nooteboom, trust must be taken as a four-part predicate: the trustor (1) trusts a trustee (2) in one or more aspects of behaviour (3) under certain circumstances (4).[7] Trustees can be individuals or collectives such as organizations or institutions.

In entrepreneurial activity, trust matters because of the ever-present relational risk.[8] Entirely risk-averse behaviour pre-empts efficient business participation. Trust can reduce the transaction costs of enforcing honest behaviour. Trust between parties permits actions to occur without extreme rigidity and expense of hierarchical organization designed to prevent the exploitation of vulnerability through labyrinthine regulations.[9] Moreover, trust may even be seen as a cooperative, constitutive value: its presence can incite reciprocity of the value, further minimizing inefficient allocation of effort and time in the marketplace.

Virtually all transactions premise upon an element of trust, especially those extended over a significant duration. Institutional activity relies upon reassuring potential customers of the institution's trustworthiness Trust-implying behaviour contributes to the emotional and cognitive foundation of trust.[10] This behaviour is fomented within relationships occurring either on a personal basis or in more impersonal methods through the representation of institutions.[11]

A barrier to participation, active distrust arises in several forms. Clients unfamiliar with microcredit operations may question the counter-intuitive nature of the process resulting from their lack of collateral. A history with exploitative credit sources also paves the way for initial distrust, with potential clients suspicious of the motives of a credit-lending institution. In areas familiar with the microcredit process, however, new institutions or new outreach by old institutions must surmount the wariness of potential clients who feel they already know what institutions have to offer: these individuals may have already declared their institutional loyalties, or have settled on non-participation based on various institutional pitfalls. To the latter point, it must be noted that research demonstrates that the poor are often distrustful of and intimidated by formal bank structures.[12] Many may be reliant on the informal savings mechanisms available to them out of familiarity, and are hesitant to switch sources despite significant benefits. Facilitating trust is necessary for any expansion of microcredit activity.

The importance of the multi-faceted quest for trust-building speaks to the 'social-embeddedness' of market transactions.[13] Participation in entrepreneurial activity is only possible if institutional and environmental factors translate to an establishment of trust, regardless of the potential economic benefit of credit access. Economic activity is thus necessarily shaped by the social interactions of agents, and the overall network of relations that governs the existence of potential and current clients. It has been argued that much of global economic backwardness can be explained by the lack of mutual confidence.[14] An absence of trust is especially prevalent in developing and transitional economies, where transactions have had a history of corruption that colours all subsequent transactions. Moreover, decision-makers in these countries often face considerable uncertainty fuelled by rapidly changing economic conditions and political instability.[15] For example, civilian upheaval as a result of social or political unrest translates to changing household dynamics as well as disruption of human, social, physical, financial and natural capital. A general disrespect for the rule of law increases the threat of theft and corruption, making households and businesses vulnerable to loss. Situational unrest has socioeconomic impacts such as unstable food supply because of insecurity in agricultural production, or rapid growth in informal sectors due to lack of opportunity. Political uncertainty also prevents stable planning for the future; this greatly erodes an individual's capability and incentive to create long-term entrepreneurial ventures.[16] Consequently, situations of tumult are characterized by the lack of confidence to build, a difficulty in viewing the future with confidence, an absence of security and fear of crisis repetition. These sentiments perpetuate a general atmosphere of distrust. In zones of general unrest, such as Pakistan, institutions have an imperative to foment trust, especially as general institutional trust erodes.

Dire situations, however, may also lower the amount of trust needed to participate: the risk-trust balancing equation turns upon the idea of prohibitive costs in potential transactions. If microcredit participation represents the only or the best mode of accessing sorely needed capital, then the barriers to obtaining trust will be lowered. This speaks to the fourth part of Nooteboom's trust predicate dictating specific circumstances in which trust will be allocated.[17] Many developing countries thus occupy a unique trust-space, in which trust is manifested more greatly in personalized relationships than in institutional relationships. As Simmel noted, similarity reassures.[18] Establishing commonality forms a basis for rapport and trust.

Institutions thus have a two-fold mission in establishing trust: they must establish both personalized and institutional trust in order to have resonance with the groups they seek to target. Concentrating solely upon personalized trust has the potential for tapping into negative social capital, which can lock people into closed, localized, cohesive communities that keep them from opening to wider perspectives of development. Peer pressure best exemplifies the nature of negative social capital. Though peer pressure can positively work to ensure timely repayment and discipline, peer pressure can also reinforce patriarchal or oppressive cultural norms, denying space for mobility of free choice. To that effect, microcredit providers must elicit trust through personal means as well as institutional avenues, all the while staying true to their nature as an institution dedicated to the enhancement of capabilities.

Establishing personal trust is dealt with quite often through Grameen's model. Grameen pioneered a model in which individuals were used as conduits of information to tap into communities: though this is an effective method of building personalized trust, its pitfalls will be discussed in more detail in the subsequent chapter. Both Kashf and Grameen use the outreach of loan officers to entrench this personalized trust, ideally allowing for sustained participation through trust-building over a period of time. This, however, does not address the question of trust at inception.

On what bases should this trust be elicited? According to Luhmann, familiarity is the primary precondition for trust.[19] That is, trust requires a degree of cognitive familiarity. Potential clients must know of the service, institution, or actor to be trusted. To develop this knowledge, institutions must move from a stage where potential clients are totally ignorant, or even misinformed, to a psychological state of comfort and knowledge. On the cognitive level of experience, trust manifests itself when individuals no longer desire further evidence or rational convincing for assuming the risk in relying on another. Marketing is one way of efficiently achieving familiarity. Through depictions and advertising in the public sphere, potential borrowers may familiarize themselves with at least the name and presence of the institution.

Understanding the acquisition of trust is possible through two distinct conceptions: the antecedent factors of trust and the base factors of trust. Antecedent factors of trust speak to factors determining the pre-existence of trust between two actors. Mayer describes the antecedents of trust as benevolence, integrity, and ability.[20] Benevolence refers to the extent which the trustee is believed to want to help the trustor, colouring the relationship as one of positive assistance. This is assumed of many microcredit institutions, provided potential clients have prior awareness of microcredit; however, we have already discussed those situations in which microcredit institutions have been accused of being fronts for other agendas. As a result, effective marketing and promotion may entrench this antecedent value of trust. Integrity refers to the trustor perceiving that the trustee adheres to a set of principles that the trustor finds acceptable and, hopefully, commendable. Strengthening the belief in institutional integrity is possible through conveying and crystallizing the institutional identity. Benevolence and integrity speak directly to perception, and not to assessment of capability. Ability, by contrast, is an assessment of an institution's success in accomplishing tasks related to its technical area. For prospective clients, this is often established and verified through assessments derived from social networks, or anecdotal evidence. This antecedent value of trust is most prone to attack: it can be presented as factual, and its subsequent damage to trust is least easily dismissed as a result. To that effect, institutions attempting to strengthen their antecedent values of trust should work to enhance their perception of benevolence and integrity.

The bases of trust draw upon environmental, existing process-oriented assessments of behaviour. For example, one base of trust is inherent, institutionally sourced trust. As noted above, this is not relevant in the developing country context: if anything, there is a base of distrust for institutions. Another base of trust is that the trustee is as an entity, or characteristic-based trust. Though similar to integrity, characteristic-based trust is process-oriented in that it indicates that the institution actually acts in a positive manner, rather than whether or not it acts in accordance with its stated ideals.[21] Characteristic-based trust speaks directly to the institutional identity and its compatibility with the potential client's own personality. So, for example, characteristic-based trust may arise from ethnic similarity, particularly because common social and cultural norms may make a satisfactory exchange easier to achieve. Moreover, characteristic-based trust is a commodity rooted in inherent personality factors. Marketing intended to elucidate the specific institutional identity of an organization can attract those with similar backgrounds. Other process-oriented bases of trust include social learning and reputation as instrumental in determining a marketer's trustworthiness.[22] Social learning indicates the creation of that trust which evolves out of past experiences and prior interaction.[23] Positive dispositional attributions of both the trustee and the trustor converge in a relationship of trust. Marketing promotes specific dispositional attributes of the institution through carefully selected imagery and presentation. Moreover, as detailed further in the next chapter, marketing also selectively targets markets it perceives as having distributional attributes responsive to what the institution can provide. Reputational trust develops as trustworthiness is repeatedly demonstrated to exchange partners through concrete actions. This form of trust is acquired within the marketplace through sustained action. Zucker depicts reputation as a symbolic representation of past exchange history.[24]

# NOTES

1. J.L. Bradach, J.L. and R.G. Eccles, 'Markets versus hierarchies: From ideal types to plural forms', *Annual Review of Sociology* (Vol 15, 1984): 97–118.
2. Ibid., 99.
3. Ibid., 103.
4. E.H. Lorenz, 'Neither friends nor strangers: informal networks of subcontracting in French industry' in D. Gambetta (ed.), *Trust: Making and Breaking Cooperative Relations* (Oxford: Basil Blackwell, 1988): 194–210.
5. M. Deutsch, 'Cooperation and trust: Some theoretical notes', in M.R. Jones (ed.), *Nebraska Symposium on Motivation* (University of Nebraska Press: Lincoln, Nebraska, 1962), 275–319.
6. Deutsch, op. cit., 296.
7. Bart Nooteboom, *Trust: forms, foundations, functions, failures and figures* (Cheltenham UK:Edward Elgar, 2002).
8. P. Dasgupta, 'Trust as a commodity' in D. Gambetta (ed.), *Trust: Making and Breaking Cooperative Relations* (Oxford: Basil Blackwell, 1988): 49–72.
9. Dasgupta, op. cit., 51.
10. Niklas Luhmann, 'Familiarity, confidence, trust', in: D. Gambetta (ed.), *Trust-making and breaking of cooperative relations*. (Oxford: Blackwell, 1988): 94–108.
11. Dominic Furlong, 'The Conceptualization of Trust in Economic Thought'. Institute of Development Studies Working Paper Series (Sussex, 1996).
12. J.D. Lewis and A.J. Weigert, 'Social atomism, holism and trust', *The Sociological Quarterly* (Vol. 26(4), 1985): 455–71.
13. Mark Granovetter, 'Economic action and social structure: the problem of embeddedness', *American Journal of Sociology* (Vol. 91, 1985): 481–510.
14. Scott Shapiro, 'The social control of impersonal trust'. *American Journal of Sociology* (Vol. 93, 1987): 623–58.
15. Hasan Bano-Burki, Shama Mohammad, 'Mobilizing Savings from the Urban Poor', ShoreBank International (Chicago: Shore Bank, January 2008).
16. N.H. Leff, 'Trust, envy, and the political economy of industrial development: economic groups in developing countries'. Columbia

First Boston Series in Money, Economics, and Finance Working Paper, (November 1986): 36–88.

17. Nooteboom, op. cit.

18. Georg Simmel, *The sociology of Georg Simmel* (Glencoe, Illinois: The Free Press, 1950).

19. Luhmann, op. cit.

20. Roger Mayer, James H. Davis, and F. David Schoorman, 'An integrative model of organizational trust', *Academy of Management Review* (Vol. 20, 1995): 709–34.

21. Luhmann, op. cit.

22. Haider Ali and Sue Birley, 'The role of trust in the marketing activities of entrepreneurs establishing new ventures'. *Journal of Marketing Management* [Volume 14(7), 1998]: 749–63.

23. Luhmann, op. cit.

24. Lynne G. Zucker, 'Production of trust: institutional sources of economic structure', in B.M. Staw (ed.), *Research in Organisational Behaviour* (Vol. 8, 1986).

CHAPTER NINE
# On Marketing and Empowerment

All outreach depends upon garnering and keeping the trust of potential clients: as microcredit providers, whether established or new ventures, are concerned with outreach, the issue of acquiring trust becomes a high priority. Mentioned in the last chapter, familiarity is needed to establish this trust, which then feeds personalized and institutional trust. In this chapter, we will examine marketing and branding as a means of establishing trust through familiarity. Moreover, we will examine how marketing, in stimulating outreach ultimately leading to higher competition, increases the efficiency of microcredit providers and creates more suitable, market-responsive options for clients.

Though the recipient of prominent global campaigns, microcredit still has room for expansion in many developing countries as credit outreach and market penetration has not yet reached all. In Pakistan, for example, a survey associated with the Human Development Report assessed that only 35.6 per cent of households had access to loans. Thus, microcredit expansion is in its early stages in Pakistan, even in urban centres with high coverage: Kashf's operating area of Lahore has the highest market penetration, reaching 13 per cent of the market.[1] Low market coverage means that there is a wealth of untapped territory; often, this is the cause of a lack of concentration on marketing programmes, as new market segments are easily identified and serviced.

The proliferation and expanded outreach of pro-poor lending institutions in Lahore has brought with it new challenges; some of the emerging issues are reports of overlapping areas of operation among microfinance providers. As a result of expanded, aggressive outreach procedures, clients have capitalized on competition or exploited opportunities by maintaining simultaneous relationships with these institutions: 'in competitive markets they are exercising choice with unflinching regularity...and many are deserting their service provider to try another or simply to take a 'rest' from the rigours of MFIs' terms and conditions.'[2]

One would imagine that increased choices would be in line with the capabilities approach to empowerment, allowing flexibility and freedom in one's participation in financial activity. In its current manifestation, however, the increase in overlapping outreach areas and subsequent competition heralds a behavioural shift for microcredit institutions. Previously, many organizations enjoyed near monopolies, operating in large, untapped areas in the second-largest urban centre in Pakistan. Now, however, expansion is accompanied by a descent into unhealthy competition. Specifically, the rising incidence of multiple-institution borrowing and the growth in attrition rate has resulted in 'client poaching' initiatives spearheaded by field staff. These group hijacking tactics include posting of field staff outside group meetings of borrowers belonging to competitor microcredit institutions, in order to persuade them to shift patronage; hiring competitor microcredit institution's field staff to access their associated borrowers; and offering incentives such as monetary benefits to clients managing borrower groups. Such tactics undermine the results of healthy competition, which ostensibly would be an environment in which borrowers could freely choose the institutions best suited to their needs, without the interference of deceptive practices. In sampled communities where four or more MFIs operate, however, many clients could only name the microcredit provider from which they obtain a loan. Outreach has thus not reached a level of overlap in which clients are dabbling in a variety of different services to determine which best suits their needs. Moreover, this means that client poaching initiatives disproportionately and unevenly target certain subsets of the population, leaving others to remain unaware of their options.

Importantly, loan officers and other field staff are integral to the success of microcredit providers.[3] As discussed earlier, it is their persistent, constant contact with borrowers which cements the personalized trust necessary in developing and high-conflict areas. Physical, face-to-face outreach characterizes the daily operations of these loan officers as they communicate with current and potential client communities. Door-to-door promotion is a common method of reaching households within targeted outreach communities; in this way, loan officers simultaneously make clients feel comfortable by venturing into their territory, and also glean important environmental and contextual information that facilitates better, more efficient operation. For building trust in the institution, field staff can help to disambiguate causality in the interpretation of microcredit-related events, separating mishaps, lack of competence and opportunism.

These same staffers also juggle multiple responsibilities that include client screening, appraisal, loan disbursement and loan monitoring, in addition to their outreach responsibilities. As field staff is tempted to invest their time in client hijacking practices, they increasingly delegate client identification, mobilization, screening and selection processes to selected contacts within the borrowing community.[4] Diverting loan officers' attention to 'poaching' clients thus severely inhibits their ability to concentrate on their primary role of facilitating access to the larger institution and synthesizing contextual practice with capabilities-oriented ideology.

The pressures to enhance outreach are perfectly under-standable; however, we must develop a strategy in which field staff can simultaneously enhance outreach and cultivate healthy, trust-building relationships with client communities. This desire to improve outreach must be balanced with the client's interest by providing her a plurality of choice, either through product diversity or by availability of differently-oriented institutions. Employing efficient, targeted marketing strategies to shape the competitive market seems instrumental to this end. Marketing allows for client familiarity with different institutions. Marketing also conveys messages about institutional identity, allowing clients to select an institution best suited to their particular needs of empowerment, access and support. Moreover, marketing performs outreach functions without monopolizing the inter-personal efforts of field staff.

Marketing, in increasing outreach, will translate to heightened competition: as marketing bestows increased awareness of options to clients in operating areas, it will naturally lead to increase in competition for these clients' patronage. That said, competition should not be ascribed negatively. Instead, competition should be seen as advantageous to the efficiency and capability of microcredit institutions.

For example, the growth in competition translates to growing numbers of institutions seeking to better understand their clients' needs and preference.[5] In attuning services to their customer base, institutions must invest significant time and resources in understanding client operating demands. This is the only means of creating tailored products and customized, directed support. Moreover, this form of market analysis ensures that the services provision process is collaborative through a constant focus on clients' demands and preferences. In framing outreach in this way, targeted marketing allows for increased portfolio size as outreach moves from being concerned solely with breadth of accessibility to also incorporating the importance of depth of applicability. An efficient marketing programme also allows the institution to analyse customer behaviour so that potential problems can be pre-empted before they lead to attrition. Similarly, consumer analysis also allows institutions to identify causes for low repayment rates so appropriate solutions can be put in place. Consistent, sustained marketing can also assist in relaying the terms and conditions of new products: marketing initiatives can transmit information regarding changes and updates to client communities. This prevents the limited or lagging understanding of available products and services, and thus enhances their use.

Marketing also gives institutions insight into the demands of the operating environment, beyond the client's individual preferences. Importantly, marketing programmes allow institutions to monitor competing groups, analysing their client impact and adjusting their own efforts to remain relevant. Marketing strategies can also highlight factors affecting the local economy, such as weather, religious holidays or cultural occasions that often impact the clients' demand for financial products or their ability to repay their loans. An emphasis on analysing political and regulatory factors allows the institution to pre-emptively prepare itself for policies, regulations or shifts that may affect their operations. Broad marketing research can also equip institutions with general knowledge on how to deal with external shocks and crises, and how they impact product demand and profitability. In short, an institutionalized marketing strategy better prepares the institution for both initial outreach as well as sustained market response, thus substantially improving its own operations.

Competition also greatly benefits clients. As a result of the market-led strategies elaborated above, competitive pressure to retain current borrowers results in an adjustment of products and procedures to better meet client preferences. One method of doing this is by reducing the transaction and opportunity cost to the borrower. The most common adjustment in service terms is speedy loan disbursement, longer repayment periods and efficient delivery channels that have lower transaction costs for the borrower. Improved response time and speedier loan disbursements also redress many of the criticisms of current MFI practices. Moreover, to sustain the competitive outreach environment, institutions will likely diversify their portfolios to service less competitive market segments, thus motivating a search for new, unserviced vicinities in an existing area of operation. This also targets the 'hard-core' poor as well as other markets that may opt out of the microcredit phenomenon for a variety of reasons, and leads to their incorporation and consideration in future outreach efforts.

Most importantly for clients, however, is the importance of competition and marketing in advertising the host of choices available to them. Without effective marketing, borrowers are not aware of other loan-giving institutions in any meaningful way. Awareness of the presence of other MFIs is insufficient: potential borrowers should be thoroughly informed about the differences in the terms and conditions offered by MFI competitors. Information on these topics is readily available, but not instantaneously accessible to those who are working in overlapping operating areas. Effective marketing, however, will make these differences apparent. Various service models will resonate in different ways to clients: ranging from pure financial assistance and business counselling to products that come packaged with education and gender training, the availability of a variety of models will allow borrowers to settle on those best suited to them. Borrowers should have complete choice freedom in selecting the services that are most applicable to their circumstances, allowing them to tailor their own path to empowerment on their own terms.

Marketing methods should be used to provide information of products and services equally to all potential clients, regardless of their situationally-impacted access to service knowledge. Marketing relies heavily on the adaptation and coordination of product, price, promotion and place for achieving effective response from potential customers.[6] Managing this marketing requires analysis, planning, implementation and the control of programmes designed to elicit exchanges with target audiences. Many institutional factors converge in an effective institutional marketing programme: loan officer management, resources for media production and incentive schemes are just a few. Internal management issues are also of the utmost importance. Few MFIs have developed formal marketing programmes: to do so would require appropriate financial and human resources, as well as a cohesive, well-researched strategy. Though marketing is obviously necessary in completely new markets, developing growth markets often omit focus on promotion because demand is large enough to compensate for gaps in outreach methodology. As outreach increases, however, and as markets become more saturated, effective marketing strategies serve as the only means of garnering more clients and retaining current ones.

The current marketing strategy employed by many institutions is the community-contact model. In establishing an individual or select group as community representatives, distribution of information can be efficient; however, there is also great potential for misinformation. These representatives carry the potential for inadvertent misrepresentation of MFI products and services. Moreover, these established resources possess a great deal of leverage and bargaining power which can manifest itself in a variety of ways. For example, it is not difficult to imagine a liaison having a bad interaction with an MFI's management or officer, and then working to prevent others' cooperation with that institution. These community contacts are in a prime position to attack the antecedent trust value of 'ability', as discussed earlier, and thus well-equipped to destroy trust in a particular institution. With pernicious 'client poaching' on the rise, institutions must reinforce themselves to guard against such damaging possibilities.

The community-contact model can also exacerbate detrimental intersections with inter-community dynamics. Though the lead community contacts are useful in making initial inroads into a community, this approach creates a hierarchy at odds with a service philosophy dedicated to access for all. Ultimately, microfinance philosophy embodies an ethos dedicated to overall enhancement of capabilities and choices, rather than the concentration of power in ways that reinforce community power hierarchies. Microcredit institutions must not contribute to the consolidation of power in the hands of few, which can be the case if certain community members are established as fixed liaisons for information dispersal in client communities. Instead, MFIs must allow for dynamism in leadership in order to prevent this sort of power consolidation. Opportunities should be made easily accessible to all, but these can be difficult to provide if the process relies on the representative powers of certain community individuals.

An effective, tailored marketing strategy should neither leave the institution open to attack, nor perpetuate patterns of community domination. In general, marketing strategies are informed by two major concepts: the product-oriented model and the selling-oriented conceptual framework.

In the product approach, the focus of the MFI is to provide services of the highest quality. Based on their experience in the field, many MFIs are tailoring and tweaking their product selection to better suit their clientele. In short, the seller creates products and services for existing wants, rather than attempting to alter attitude and demand to fit the existing supply of products. This structure restores client sovereignty:[7] it is the client's needs that determine the nature of assistance, rather than others paternalistically determining what would best suit her path out of poverty. Demand-sensitive product creation allows clients to select the product mix provided by MFIs. This is in keeping with the independent, self-sufficiency oriented ethos of microcredit. The product approach does, however, have potential pitfalls: new products may be introduced not because of a market demand or strong need, but instead because peer institutions are launching such products. The impulse to keep up with competition in the product realm may ultimately be an inefficient allocation of resources for a variety of situational, financial and infrastructural reasons. Such competitive creation of products is especially treacherous for MFIs with limited resources.

By contrast, the selling approach focuses on persuading potential customers to buy the services being provided. In contrast to the market-led product creation approach, the sales orientation finds customers for existing products, and then promotes the sale of these products.[8] The mode is often simple, person-to-person outreach spearheaded by a team of loan officers. Loan officers contact local point persons to assist in the selling process. Thus, marketing largely devolves into the responsibility of a local point person to acquire new borrowers and re-attract old clients to buy the offered products. All information on service availability, product features, terms and conditions is distributed through these channels. In doing so, other MFIs face difficulty 'breaking into' a given market, as information is controlled often by prominent community figures; such an arrangement obscures the presence of other competitive MFIs who may provide services well-suited or attractive to the community at hand. In a more effective selling approach, a marketing team should make use of market segmentation analysis even within the relatively narrow base of the poor in need of microcredit services. Unique selling programmes should be designed for young, single women, women ultimately seeking education, new mothers, mothers with many children, women in areas with heavily gendered access to mobility, those women who have more capability to move around, etc. Within the market segment of the poor who could potentially benefit from microcredit, there still exist different positions and situations: a one-size-fits-all approach is woefully reductionist, and does not acknowledge the dynamism or diversity even within those facing poverty. In learning what sells to these individual segments, marketers will necessarily learn what clients want.

In practice, most marketing efforts represent a mixture of selling and product creation. Effective and creative use of the media can assist with both approaches as well as help in surmounting barriers to information dispersal and successful outreach. At present, media is rarely used aside from distribution of printed pamphlets during sales calls or when these pamphlets are given to the local resource persons for distribution amongst their peers. Relying upon word of mouth and personal outreach is a useful tactic, especially in areas of low literacy, but dynamic use of media as a marketing tool should supplement these initiatives.

Marketing of microfinance is not exactly analogous to the selling of services and products; instead, it markets an entire ethos and philosophy. For example, Grameen's presentation of the Sixteen Decisions along with its product indicates that the process is not merely a market transaction of services, but rather a promotion of a complete mode of life. As a result, those crafting a strategy for microcredit institutions should look to the ideals of social marketing for guidance. Social marketing is 'the design, implementation, and control of programs seeking to increase the acceptability of a social idea or practice in a target group(s).'[9] Using social marketing as a framework can identify potential problems with designed initiatives: for example, Kotler highlights that social marketing often has little flexibility in shaping products or offerings.[10] Once dedicated to a particular image, social marketing programmes often find themselves locked into a given social behaviour that cannot be modified or changed. In the microcredit sphere, for example, this may mean that the government requires MFIs to use only training and sensitivity classes to approach gender relations issues. As most MFIs have general poverty alleviation as their stated and intended goal, more flexibility is allowed to their marketing initiatives so long as external interference is prevented from influencing the adoption of specific tactics. Additionally, the presence of the loan officers and constant individual attention allows institutions to uniquely tailor their marketing agenda on a continuous basis.

The effectiveness of social campaigns is dependent on the client's experience with several factors.[11] When these factors are analysed in terms of microfinance relevance, it seems that social campaign-oriented marketing is quite pertinent. The first is the force or the intensity of the person's motivation towards the goal. This is measured through a combination of her predisposition prior to the message and the stimulating effect of the message. As the goal of many institutions is to reduce poverty and facilitate consumption, this seems to be an end to which many will be predisposed. The resultant stimulation caused by the message is more complex, as it must successfully grapple with the initial counter-intuitiveness most people have for microcredit schemes, particularly those who are accustomed to exclusion from the credit market or exploitative loan sharking from informal sources. All marketing initiatives must keep in mind this potential obstacle to getting a successful response. The second factor is the direction of the message: it must convey the knowledge of how or where a person might go for help to realize this motivation; that is, it must be clear how to begin this process. Social marketing must make an institution's role, location and easy accessibility explicitly clear. The third factor is the mechanism, or the existence of agency in enabling the potential client to translate motivation into action. It must be abundantly clear that this is plausible and accessible to all who can access the marketing message. The fourth factor is institutional adequacy, or the trust that the institution in question is capable of performing its task. This speaks to issues of institutional trust, which we will touch upon shortly. Many microcredit dispensing groups do not instantaneously garner trust, especially as more and more such institutions come into existence. Without such trust, no marketing message will be successful. Of the five factors indicating the success of social marketing, this is the trickiest. The final factor is distance, or the client's estimate of the energy and cost required to enact and actualize what is being marketed. Institutions should be encouraged to have readily accessible offices and branches, which many do. Importantly, however, the ambience of these branches must be friendly in order to eliminate or minimize the psychological distance between a potential client and an institution.

Thus, social marketing orientations will succeed when they are based on sensitivity to the perceptions, needs and wants of target markets, and when they satisfy these through the design, communication, pricing and delivery of appropriate and competitively viable offerings.[12] Tactics employed to implement social marketing strategies coupled with a market-responsive product expansion will increase profitability by enhancing customer loyalty.[13]

To determine a successful social marketing strategy, then, MFIs must create a trustworthy, distilled representation of its identity and vision. In high-competition areas this becomes even more significant: potential clients need shorthand indicators of the differences amongst institutions. With meaningful differences difficult to find, potential clients look for signals in seemingly trivial factors: the appearance of the banking hall, the behaviour of the front-line staff and other non-explicit cues of suitability. A carefully constructed brand can better project the personality and offerings of an MFI.

A brand is defined as a 'name, term, symbol or design intended to signify the goods and services of one seller to differentiate them from those of competitors.'[14] Brands help create value and produce meaning for an MFI, dependent on compelling visual rhetoric.[15] Images are especially powerful in that they convey a sense that one 'knows places, times, and peoples that we have never experienced.'[16] Images in marketing communication serve as a proxy for experience, especially when other information sources are subject to contest.[17] Even more importantly, images serve as a foundation for future attempts to comprehend and construct environmental changes. Thus, images in marketing communication play cultural as well as persuasive roles, functioning as cultural text.[18] Often, these triggers are automatic and without awareness.[19] Brands can function as transformative devices, eliciting trust from consumers as the history, experience and personality of an institution are juxtaposed into one particular image.

A successful brand has several important qualities. Most importantly, the brand must have instant recognition. This allows consumers to feel they know what to expect, and know what to ask for when seeking services. In the MFI context, this is very important: this establishes trust through repeated familiarization. Recognition also serves as a marker for differentiation so that the well-branded MFI is distinguished from the crowd of competitors. A brand must have credibility, so consumers can believe in the institution's capacity for acting on its promises. This is particularly important for those organizations offering savings services, as clients who previously have not interacted with formal institutions controlling their finances may feel hesitant.[20] Brands must also convey warranty of the quality and reliability of services offered by the MFI. All these factors facilitate promotion, since promotion efforts then monopolize less time of the loan officers and allow for resources to be diverted to emphasizing the MFI's competitive advantages and products in a personalized setting, after the brand prevalence has addressed the precursor concerns. A brand can also facilitate word-of-mouth advertising, as it provides a reference point for conversations about the services offered by an institution. Customers can easily recommend the MFI and its services by referring to a commonly known image brand. Those hearing the recommendation can also more readily remember the information if it refers to a familiar image. The brand creates an association with a particular set of features and standards by enabling and facilitating recognition, credibility and reliability.

Identity is the strategic heart of the brand: it entails what the MFI imagines the brand to be, and how it translates the experience and offerings of the MFI. This invokes institutional identity by embodying the unique characteristics of the MFI. These factors, including the culture, strategy, structure and appearance, converge to form a definition of that institution's cumulative past, present and future. In developing this institutional identity, it is crucial to ensure consistency so that the customers' experience of the MFI and its identity is the same irrespective of which branch they visit. This identity then informs the brand image, which reflects specifically the psychological aspects of the brand: how it resonates with consumers, and what responses it elicits.[21] The cultural meaning of the brand is acquired through the influence and presentation of employees, product category associations, the types of users typically associated with it, distribution practices and its inherent symbolism.[22]

In creating this successful brand, MFIs must not only have in-depth and detailed knowledge of their potential client base, as they would derive through a marketing strategy, but they must also concretely identify and crystallize their own image to appropriately characterize their brand. These only strengthen the incentive to analyse client preferences, and clearly demarcate client segments. Moreover, the MFI is forced to identify its competitive advantage and the advantages it wishes to promote given its target market's needs and expectations. To understand positive and negative motivators for value and to then translate those into a brand requires deep knowledge of client preferences. To employ the brand, the MFI must systematically build awareness of their representation, in addition to promoting their offered products and services.

In terms of imagery, Grameen's brand successfully evokes a dedication to its promoted corporate identity. First, Grameen has cultivated a mythology of individual motivation and empowerment: stories of Muhammad Yunus' enthusiastic initiative to single-handedly create the Grameen enterprise reflect his belief that small-scale entrepreneurship is the ideal mode for empowerment. This psychological imagery and belief conveys a strong faith in ones ability to pull oneself out of poverty. The Grameen brand logo evokes a dedication to this belief. As a bank, the institution must convey strategic banking values of stability, strength and security. Each value has a psychological dimension in reinforcing Grameen's dedication to the power of the individual. For example, stability is expressed in visual form by a sturdy green house, metaphorically referencing long-term endurance.[23] The use of a single, solid image without distracting details evokes strength through its bold, graphic depiction. Finally, selecting an image of a sturdy home, rather than the shanties or informal structures that many of the impoverished inhabit, represents security. A home with four walls and a roof indicates that the owner has withstood economic tribulations and tumult. In this way, security relates to psychological anxiety about financial matters. Using a home demonstrates that Grameen Bank is not merely a depository of money, but also a repository of one's hopes and dreams.[24] The resonance and ubiquity of this name brand has allowed Grameen to cultivate trust in its product, and to capitalize on this trust to diversify into myriad industries. This further perpetuates the self-referential stability of Grameen's brand logo. Grameen continues to spread its stability and entrepreneurship-oriented message by its involvement in a variety of business sectors. By establishing itself in telecommunications, textiles, energy and the like, Grameen created an empire based on a name brand synonymous with the enabling individuals to attain stability and security.

Building familiarity through branding, as Grameen has successfully done, assists in building trust. Without trust, neither the MFI nor the subsequent entrepreneurial activity can continue.[25] Trust forms the basis of a positive brand reputation, or a belief that the brand guarantees stability, reliability, and competence in its delivery of service. If presented properly, the brand will appeal to a market of consumers who choose its products over those of competitors because of how applicable and appropriate these are for their needs.[26] Especially important for microcredit, it is just the promise of stability that a prospective client initially has when choosing to embark on microcredit activities. Eliciting large amounts of consumer trust thus contributes to a sustainable competitive advantage in outreach and growth.[27]

This trust is especially pertinent in situations of uncertainty. The idea of uncertainty has two functional levels especially in the context of the Pakistani environment: not only is there an issue of economic insecurity in the target markets, hence the selling of credit products, but there is also an issue of large-scale political instability which often translates to a distrust of institutions. Brands can work to transcend that instability by promoting an image of security. Using the brand and associated media to express institutional commitment is more accessible and more stable than solely relying on interpersonal recruitment, especially in times of unrest. Importantly, branding, in defining an institution, indicates some semblance of institutional permanence. This translates to an expectation of responsibility to a particular representational image. In referencing a history of dedication, branding evokes the ideal imagery necessary for marketing microcredit in areas of instability and transition. Different institutions will encapsulate their institutional identity and history in distinct ways, and in doing so, will appeal to diverse markets. The brand operates by simultaneously transmitting information about the institution, which allows field staff to emphasize substantive interpersonal trust-building contact, and enables clients to choose the services best tailored to help in attaining eventual empowerment.

# NOTES

1. Irfan Aleem, 'Imperfect Information, Screening, and the Costs of Informal Lending: A Study of a Rural Credit Market in Pakistan'. *World Bank Economic Review* (Vol. 4, 1990).
2. Bano-Burki and Mohammad, op. cit.
3. Aleem, op. cit.
4. B.S. Morewagae, M. Seemule, & H. Rempel, 'Access to credit for non-formal micro-enterprises in Botswana', *Journal of Development Studies* [Volume 31(3), 1995]: 481–504.
5. Bano-Burki and Mohammad, op. cit.
6. Zucker, op. cit.
7. Ezra Anyango, Jennefer Sebstad, and Monique Cohen, 'Assessment of the Use and Impact of MicroSave's Market Research for MicroFinance Toolkit' (Nairobi: Microsave, 2002).
8. Philip Kotler, *Marketing Management: Analysis, Planning and Control.* Second Edition (Englewood Cliffs, N.J.: Prentice-Hall, Inc., 1972).
9. Ibid.
10. Philip Kotler and Gerald Zaltman, 'Social Marketing: An Approach to Planned Social Change', *Journal of Marketing* (Vol. 35, No. 3, 1971): 3–12.
11. Philip Kotler, *Marketing Management: Analysis, Planning and Control.* Second Edition (Englewood Cliffs, N.J.: Prentice-Hall, Inc., 1972).
12. Ibid., 59.
13. Ibid., 63.
14. Craig Churchill and Sarah Halpern, 'Building Customer Loyalty: A Practical Guide for Microfinance Institutions' (Washington: Microfinance Network, 2001).
15. Ibid.
16. Barbara J. Phillips and Edward McQuarrie (ed.), *Go Figure: New Directions in Advertising Rhetoric* (Armonk, NY: M.E. Sharpe, 2007).
17. Kotler, op. cit., 12.
18. Jonathan Schroeder, Jonathan E., 'Consuming Representation: A Visual Approach to Consumer Research in Representing Consumers', in Barbara B. Stern (ed.) *Voices, Views, and Visions* (New York: Routledge, 1998): 193–230.
19. E. Delgodo-Ballester and J.L. Munuera-Alemán, 'Brand trust in the context of consumer loyalty'. *European Journal of Marketing* (Vol. 35, 2001):1238–58.

20. Phillips and McQuarrie, op. cit.
21. John Bargh, 'Losing Consciousness: Automatic Influences on Consumer Judgment, Behavior, and Motivation'. *Journal of Consumer Research* (Vol. 29, 2002): 280–5.
22. Stuart Rutherford, 'Money Talks: Conversations with Poor Households in Bangladesh about Managing Money'. Institute of Development Policy and Management (Manchester: University of Manchester, 2002).
23. Jonathan Schroeder and Miriam Salzer-Morling, *Brand Culture* (London: Routledge, 2006).
24. John Onians, *Bearers of Meaning: The Classical Orders in Antiquity, the Middle Ages, and the Renaissance* (Cambridge: Cambridge University Press, 1988).
25. Phillips and McQuarrie, op. cit.
26. Harry Beckwith, *Selling the Invisible: A Field Guide to Modern Marketing* (USA: Warner Books, 1997).
27. Rajeev Batra, 'The Situational Impact of Brand Image Beliefs', *Journal of Consumer Psychology* (14:3, 2004): 318–30.

# CONCLUSION

Increased outreach carries with it two divergent implications. First, outreach speaks to the general success of an institution. Greater outreach means either that the institution is helping more individuals in need, or is approaching self-sustainable levels quickly. Second, outreach leads to heightened competition among institutions in overlapping operating areas. Negatively characterized, this competition leads to deceptive, obstructive and misleading practices in garnering new clients. As microcredit's popularity expands, however, only two outcomes are possible: either institutions will grow monolithic, serving thousands of people, or tailored, 'boutique' style institutions will emerge to serve divergent needs. Naturally, many will frame institutional success as achieving the former, especially given the wild success of Grameen and its subsequent growth. That said, the latter situation is a more attainable model for many of the replications inspired by Grameen.

As a result, the presence of growing competition in overlapping operating areas should not be framed as a problem. Instead, it should propel a shift in focus. Rather than concentrating on the breadth of outreach, microcredit providers should promote depth with tailored approaches suited to the lives of specific subsets of women. This permits more institutional efficiency in a variety of ways, but most importantly it speaks directly to the idea of empowerment as choice freedom.

In a market characterized by a multitude of specialty-oriented microcredit providers, women are given a host of choices in terms of breaking out of poverty. This does not lead to empowerment as choice unless women are made aware of their options, and knowledgably equipped to select the most appropriate or representative of their experience. To that end, promotional strategies must be employed by microcredit providers to make women aware of their choices in the market. Institutions also benefit greatly from the information derived through market-led approaches to service and product provision. In this way, marketing encourages a cooperative, symbiotic relationship between institutions and clients, facilitating women's empowerment. This approach to empowerment resonates regardless of which model of empowerment achievement is espoused by the institution: for the financial self-sustainability groups, a more understanding collaboration leads to heightened efficiency, whereas for the feminist empowerment and poverty alleviation groups, increased tailoring means that women will have more leverage in exercising agency in society and in the household.

Marketing engenders familiarity, an element without which outreach or sustained relationships cannot thrive. Through the use of brands, marketing strategies can elicit trust in institutional stability and sustainability; moreover, this makes the institutional identity familiar to the prospective client. Grameen was successful to this end: its ubiquitous use of branding gave it enough presence in the public space to achieve public trust. Grameen inhabited public space in the village as well: the creation of a weekly meeting place serves as a highly visible and tangible reminder of the village's status as a 'Grameen village'. When women pass by this meeting place on a daily basis they are reminded of their responsibilities and newfound roles, reinforcing their desire to help themselves out of poverty. Grameen's institutionalization of itself into the daily life of the village not only makes women conscious of their obligations to group members and their families but also promotes publicity of the project throughout the village. Furthermore, the presence of a weekly meeting space also assures those people who are hesitant to join the programme that Grameen is not a 'fly-by-night', exploitative scheme, rather it is seriously committed to improving the lives of the villagers. Branding serves as a shorthand, visual reiteration of these factors. As a replicating institution, Grameen should integrate the importance of these forms of impacting the public space for those seeking to initiate a Solidarity Group Lending Model replication.

Market-responsive outreach can also overcome many of the previously discussed environmental obstacles to growth. For example, some blame religious conservatism as a barrier to microfinance growth in Pakistan. As seen in the Grameen model, reaching an understanding with religious leaders in operating areas can diffuse much of the opposition to microfinance. Similarly, institutional strategizing can prepare for environmental shocks. The environment in which Bangladeshi microfinance initially flourished was also one in which there was a dire need to cope with a major crisis caused by widespread famine; it can be hypothesized that perhaps that situation made potential clients more willing to try a revolutionary method of income generation and entrepreneurial sustenance. Institutions can prepare themselves for such situations, especially if they are invested in geographically and culturally proximate operating areas. Other barriers to growth may also be overcome through sustained presence in the public sphere, engendering enough trust so that potential clients choose to 'risk' participation.

In discussions of choice as freedom, the concentration has been on individual choice. An individual's selection of an appropriately tailored institution does facilitate her own chosen avenue of empowerment, but mentions nothing of group empowerment. Expansion in one's individual framework of agency neglects structural oppression which dictates the acceptable sphere of behaviour. Here is where the Solidarity Group Lending Model can capitalize on the enhancement of large-scale trust in microcredit institutions. As individuals begin to affiliate with institutions based on different affinity factors, bonding will grow based on common empowerment outlooks rather than on familial or geographic ties. Group solidarity lending reinforces the intertwined futures of affinity groups. As a result, solidarity moves from instrumental solidarity, or that which enables access to capital, to outcome-oriented solidarity. Solidarity among women can serve as a powerful tool for progressive social change if it can foster critiques of dominant cultural ideologies.[1] Thus, participation in these groups can promote a secure base from which such structural empowerment-oriented activities can be actualized. Tailored microcredit institutions provide a venue in which social capital can be stimulated in new ways, as their initiatives build trust among new groups of women. This trust feeds overall social capital, or the institutions, relationships, attitudes and values that govern interactions among people. In short, a growth in social capital leads to a strengthened common sense of 'civic responsibility'. This has extensive implications for social reform leading to holistic human development. Reorganizing and re-prioritizing the microcredit market allows for the ultimate actualization of the double bottom line of financial and social empowerment.

# NOTE

1. Naila Kabeer, 'The Conditions and Consequences of Choice: Reflections on the Measurement of Women's Empowerment', UNRISD Discussion Paper No. 108 (1999).

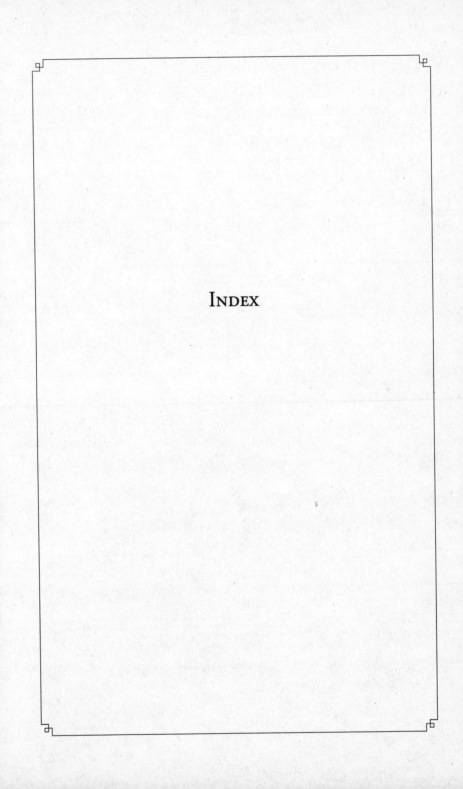

INDEX